SPIRITUAL LESSONS FOR A
YOUNG DISCIPLE

VOLUME 1
THE POWER OF FAITH

WILLIAM HAYES PINGREE

PRAETORIUS PUBLISHERS, LLC

Copyright © 2018 Praetorius Publishers, LLC

All rights reserved.

All rights reserved. No part of this publication may be reproduced, stored in a retrieval system, or transmitted, in any form or by any means, electronic or otherwise, without prior permission of Praetorius Publishers, LLC.

Library of Congress Cataloging-in-Publication Data
Pingree, William Hayes
Spiritual Lessons for a Young Disciple / Volume I / William Hayes Pingree
Library of Congress Number: 2018935442

ISBN 978-1-942298-47-2

Printed in the United States of America

First Edition

CONTENTS

INTRODUCTION   1

01 MOTIVE IS EVERYTHING   9
Why We Need the Right Motive
The Right Motive
The Wider and Deeper View of Life

02 COMMUNICATING WITH THE SAVIOR   31
Finding Relevance in the Gospel
Communicating with Real Intent
Finding Answers Through Faith

03 BEING BORN AGAIN   43
The Journey Begins with Prayer
Born of the Water and the Spirit
Walking the Path of Holiness
How to be Born Again
Spiritual Rebirth
Discovering His Will Focuses Faith

04 THE ABILITY TO SEE   63
Vanity Causes Spiritual Blindness
Faith Empowers Our Willingness to Sacrifice
Being Born of the Spirit Changes Priorities
The Example of Oliver Cowdery
Being Born Again is Rarely Theatric, but
    Always Impressive

05 THE NEED FOR A BROKEN HEART AND CONTRITE SPIRIT 83

Sacrificing the Self for the Soul
The Antidote to Pride
Esau and Jacob: Contrasting Rewards
Avoid Confusing Worldly Gains with Spiritual Gains
No Direct Link Between Riches and Obedience
The Danger of Pride

06 FAITH IS A GIFT 105

Embracing Him Through Faith
Faith Centers Our Obedience
The Universal Sin
Receiving the Savior with a Broken Heart
The Persuasive Power of Meekness
Justified by the Savior Through the Spirit

07 INCREASING OUR FAITH 127

The Unprofitable Servant
His Truth Illuminates Our Soul
The Example of the Sons of Mosiah
The Consequence of a Prideful Heart

08 FAITH AND VIRTUE 141

Faith is Both a Law and Principle
George Washington's Example
Linking Virtue with Faith
Faith Beyond the Veil
The Law of Faith is Foundational to the Soul

09 FAITH, LOVE, AND OBEDIENCE 159

The Higher Covenant of Love
Selfless Obedience Re-orders the Soul
The Requirement of His Grace
Obedience Makes Our Faith Perfect
Obedience Must be Voluntary Not Compelled
Redemptive Faith

10 HOW DOES THE LORD APPROVE OF MY SERVICE 179

True Disciples Serve with Correct Motive
The Ironies of Life and the Atonement
The Role of Justification and Sanctification
Understanding Our Relationship with Jesus Christ

EPILOGUE 191

INTRODUCTION

The purpose of these many lessons found in *Spiritual Lessons for a Young Disciple* is to set a broad framework for the doctrinal reasons why young Latter-day Saints who are about to embark on life's mission desire to find the joy of discipleship as they interact with others. These might be missionaries, fellow students, co-workers or other similarly motivated young people that desire to make a difference in our ever-more troubling world. Further, young disciples have a unique opportunity whether they be missionaries, students, or other service-minded young Latter-day Saints to teach doctrine, and the more they know the doctrines of the restoration, the better able they will be to understand the Savior's mission. Becoming a disciple of the Savior is much more than simply being a member of His church. While He rejoices in our desire to be united with other Latter-day Saints, He calls on us to rise up and embrace our spiritual inheritance; being united with Him as we stand up for His cause as a witness to His life and sacrifice.

We will come to understand His desire for others to embrace His gospel and when we come to understand this, then our desire to know Him will increase. Sometimes, as we begin to understand our relationship with both the gospel and the Church, we find it easy to combine and confuse worldly reasons for our service with spiritual reasons for building a lifelong relationship with the Lord. While the one should support the other, often we find ourselves with a lopsided view of the secular benefits found in all forms of Church service, including responding to a mission call, and yet neglect the powerful change of heart that being an active and engaged young disciple affords young men and women today.

We find that for a host of sophisticated reasons, we seek to be involved in expanding our desire to know our Savior so that we can be effective examples to others whether or not they are engaged in missionary work, volunteer work, academic life or other worthy pursuits. In such instances, our knowledge of the doctrines of the restoration become pivotal in our ability to reflect the light of our Savior to those with whom we serve; in this way, we ourselves will be blessed. And while this is indeed true, if we become devotees to behavior modification programs without a sure conviction of the mission of our Savior in our own lives, any other reasons ultimately are unsatisfactory.

Many good-intentioned people have given us varied and different opinions as to why we should want to become true disciples of Christ. These range from reasons such as enhancing our abilities in school to our ability to excel in church leadership after we have rendered exemplary service either in the mission field, at the university, in our chosen professions, or in the corporate world. In our pursuit of excellence, we may develop great organizational skills, enhance our abilities to make good decisions, and these may be invaluable to our future careers. But without an unshakeable knowledge of the mission of our Lord Jesus Christ, especially as it relates to the restoration of the gospel, this will leave our souls unfed even as the self excels. We are counseled to manage our time and thereby learn to apply these gospel principles to our coming lives, which will be of incalculable value, as we become productive members of society. Would it not also be of greatest value to know our soul is intact and our lives approved through the gift of the Holy Ghost?

The answer to this question is self-evident. To that end, we will need to be assured that our motive for any kind of service that involves our knowledge of the doctrine of Christ is pure and not selfish. If we seek for abilities to be better workers, communicators or to be more dependable in our areas of future endeavor, after our primary education is completed, we seek for that which is good. But, if we neglect food for the soul, if we think matters of the self outweigh matters of the soul, we cheat ourselves out of a rich private spiritual life, the benefits of which cannot be counted in terms of any earthly reward. While these skills that advantage the self may indeed benefit us in terms of being better and more efficient servants, they can miss the greater mark as to why we have been inspired to become disciples of the Lord in the first place.

We can learn these skills for the self without tending to the soul by enrolling in courses that teach such skills, and because these skills have intrinsic market value, such instruction would perhaps be more satisfactorily accomplished there. It is in the world and in secular education that we learn such skills as cost-benefit analysis or how to measure success by using a host of measurements. These include profit margins, numbers of sales calls, or other kinds of utilitarian measurements that if they are good, proclaim success. But if we do not tend to our soul, the real reason to become a young disciple will be in fact obscured. When such an analysis is undertaken without a desire to feed the soul, there is one common thread running through these reasons, and that is selfishness. To avoid this unfortunate condition, we must ask ourselves, "What is the motive behind our desire to be known as a young disciple?"

Being active in the service of the Lord, whether it be in missionary work, as a student or as a young member of any work force, our motive must be the love of our Lord and the knowledge that His love can heal a broken world, a broken life, a broken marriage, even a broken nation. The world needs unselfish young disciples firmly grounded in the doctrine of Christ to show the world the way to peace. Is not the Lord known as the Prince of Peace? In order to reflect His light, our motivation for any kind of service in His cause needs to be pure. Often in our world, young men and women have been exposed to great electronic tools, which are used to assist us in getting our work done. We often look to these kinds of innovations to find ways to make our work easier.

However, we must never forget that if we want to change a life, if we want to lift a soul, the human touch is required. While using modern devices to communicate is good in some ways, we need to know before we embark in any service of the Lord that face-to-face work is required. Often this work is hard work where we need to be vulnerable to the human condition; our hearts need to be moved by the condition of the world and we need to see how the Lord's gospel will alleviate the circumstances due to the fall of man. We must realize that the work of recovering the soul is hard work for all of us. Service is the key, but it must be the kind of service that is directed towards others. With respect to missionary service, President Monson has said, "Missionary work is hard work.... It is a labor of love, sacrifice, and devotion" ("Who Honors God, God Honors," *Ensign*, November 1995, page 49). Any service that is given for the benefit of the soul is demanding and requires long hours of study and preparation. Being a young disciple requires us to see our labors as a labor of love—a love that conveys to the world the unconditional grace of Christ to reach out to all. His message is one that embraces all men and women everywhere and we must be men and women who match that message regardless of the venue chosen for such service.

Therefore, as we learn to master spiritual principles, let us never forget that the secular reasons for becoming true disciples of Christ are more than serving the needs of the self, we must also serve the more important imperative: feed the soul. The secular skills that are to be acquired as a result of Christian service, for example, those that have marketability, are in fact those that pertain to the self. While these may be important reasons, they must never become the primary reason for our service. The matters that pertain to the soul are those that are most needed, and these matters, if they are the primary reasons for our service, will allow us to find ourselves in the Lord's service for the rest of our lives. They will expand our understanding of spiritual truth and provide a firm foundation for our ability to lift the downtrodden, minister to the needs of the infirm, and magnify our ability to understand our Savior and His love.

We find in James' definition of true religion the reasons for our need to minister to the matters of the soul. Said he, *"Pure religion and undefiled before God and the Father is this, To visit the fatherless and widows in their affliction, and to keep himself unspotted from the world"* (James 1:27). In a more modern version, the Weymouth New Testament, this verse is rendered, *"The religious service which is pure and stainless in the sight of our God and Father is to visit fatherless children and widowed women in their time of trouble, and to keep one's own self unspotted from the world."* If we only concern ourselves with the matters of the self and our ability to make a market out of our service as a disciple of Christ, we will not be sensitive to the needs of the poor nor of the fatherless; certainly we will not understand the plight of the widow. In this way, we may in fact be overly influenced to confuse the world with the things that actually belong to the Spirit.

We see these traits reflected in the lives of the men who have been called to direct our spiritual efforts in the world today. Who can forget President Monsen's example of visiting the widow or the sick; who is not impressed by President Benson's mission to war-torn Europe after World War II where he ministered to the needs of those who needed food in Poland, Scandinavia, Holland and Belgium? He visited the orphan and the fatherless, not to mention those who had been widowed because of the scourge of war. And then there is the ministry of President Grant who, in the face of the Great Depression, organized the welfare system that even today minister's relief to those who are in need. We see this kind of compassion in

President Hinckley's vision inspired by Brigham Young's great ability to bring those saints from Europe to Utah. Then, all Latter-day Saints contributed unmeasured sums of money to the Perpetual Emigration Fund, which brought tens of thousands of Latter-day Saints to Zion; now, due to President Hinckley's vision, Latter-day Saints contribute substantial sums to the Perpetual Education Fund so that many disadvantaged can avail themselves of educational opportunities. In this way, life will be improved.

Further, if the reasons for our service settle on the reasons found in earthly success, we do not keep ourselves unspotted from the world nor do we look after the health of our soul. We see this fact reflected not only in the lives of the prophets mentioned above, but also in the lives of other great men and women. The laws of God and the principles of the gospel are universally applicable. These lessons begin with an understanding of faith as Paul taught in Romans 10:17–18, *"And this proves that faith comes from a Message heard, and that Message comes through its having been spoken by Christ. But I ask, have they not heard? Yes, indeed: To the whole world the preachers' voices have sounded forth, and their words to the remotest parts of the earth"* (Weymouth New Testament). It is to this end that Volume I is dedicated: that we might hear His voice in the words of His legal administrators and thereby we will receive the gift of faith.

We will draw on examples in which faith can be found. God is no respecter of persons (Acts 10:34) and His laws are reflected in the lives of great leaders everywhere. The purpose of *Spiritual Lessons for a Young Disciple* is to once again establish the primary and fundamental reasons for any kind of gospel-related service. We need to come to know how to tend the soul. This is important so that we learn to serve God, and learn how the Lord interacts with us and why He is so eager to expand our understanding and to make our soul fit for the journey of life.

01
MOTIVE IS EVERYTHING

Making the decision to become a disciple of Christ should not be taken lightly. When confronted with the reality of service in the Lord's vineyard, whether that be as a full-time missionary, a volunteer, or a student places overwhelming expectations on those who choose the path of Christ. There are many reasons offered to us as to why we should become a true disciple. With so many opportunities for all kinds of service, we all bring to that service varied spiritual, economic, social, and educational backgrounds. So we must ask a fundamental question: What is the best reason to serve? In a world where there are so many benefits for such service, why is finding the right motive for our service so important? As we seek enlightenment, we quickly discover that this important truth remains: motive is everything.

Even though our life as a disciple will be filled with challenges to grow, when armed with the right motive, everything else will be for our good. What is that best motive? The only motive that provides a bedrock reason for service as a disciple is this: we need to develop an overwhelming love for the Savior and as we do, we will come to know His love for us intimately. Armed with that love, we then will see discipleship as a way by which we can deepen our commitment to Him while at the same time growing closer to that Being who has redeemed us from the woes and vicissitudes of mortal life. That very Being who has delivered us from death and hell becomes the central focus of our lives. Our love for Christ then gives us the correct motive for serving Him; all other reasons pale in comparison to this single purpose.

Motive is different than motivation; motivation implies behavior modification, which is important, but motive comes from our heart—a sense of desire to be connected to our Lord, to be one with Him. Did He not pray to the Father in John 17:11, *"And now I am no more in the world, but these are in the world, and I come to thee. Holy Father, keep through thine own name those whom thou hast given me, that they may be one, as we are."* This is the single most correct motive for any disciple to serve his or her Master. Why? It is because for us to be found laboring in the cause of Christ in this way, the Father keeps us in His own name and thereby allows us to become one with our Savior. True discipleship always involves service under all conditions. Consequently, we must find the correct motive for that service so all might be edified.

We read in Mosiah 5:13 the following, *"For how knoweth a man the master whom he has not served, and who is a stranger unto him, and is far from the thoughts and intents of his heart?"* How can we serve Him suitably if we do not love Him? Missionary service will be challenging, but armed with our love for Christ, we will embrace His doctrines and seek salvation in His plan. As we become grounded in His doctrine and learn of His ways, we will be better prepared to embrace the challenges of the life of a disciple, as well as those that we will face when our service is ended. It is necessary for each young disciple to prepare for service, as such preparation will allow young men and women to grow spiritually in ways that will allow a rich and fulfilling spiritual life that will sustain them throughout a lifetime of service in the Lord's kingdom.

A life of service, the goal of all disciples of the Savior, is a very personal endeavor, so it is important to acknowledge that many righteous individuals do not serve a mission. There are great and inspired leaders, even some prophets, who were unable to serve full-time proselyting missions, but by becoming a true disciple of the Master, they likewise learned to serve Him in an excellent way. These men and women were able to gain the knowledge and experience needed for their high church calling even without the benefit of a mission.

As these principles of discipleship unfold, one truth will become very clear: motive is everything. And it is by this standard that our actions will be measured; it will be by this standard that we will seek Him in faith, for if our motives are impure, faith becomes an impossibility. We will never be able to develop redemptive faith because impure motives cause our faith such as it is, to remain belief. As we keep our motives pure and Godlike, we will come to know that our own

> **As these principles of discipleship unfold, one truth will become very clear: motive is everything**

conversion is vital; it is the only way we can lift others to higher ground. If our motives are not pure, personal conversion may be derailed and the great growth of one's testimony that occurs in the service of the Master could be put at risk.

As we begin to seriously contemplate the concept of Christian service that embodies a mission, and as we come to realize the best motive for such service is our love of the Lord, we will begin to find intimate reasons to love Him; and then, just as did Enos (see Enos 1:13), we then will begin to comprehend the love the Savior has for all His children. After all, did not John teach us that He loved us first (1 John 4:19)? Therefore, as we contemplate service in His cause, we need to reflect His light, not ours. But first, we need to receive His light. Then, once we have received this light, we come to understand that a primary reason we have been given the unrivaled gifts of salvation and exaltation is not only for our own benefit, but for others as well. Accordingly, and without apology, we have the privilege before us to declare that love of our Savior as we have personally experienced it; as young disciples, we will have the privilege to be His witnesses throughout our lives for we will have been changed by His love. The message of His goodness and peace to a sinful and suffering world is reflected in His sacrifice for all who embrace His Atonement; this message of healing found in Christ cannot be embraced without the right motives.

Therefore, we need to be prepared to spend our entire lives in His service and find joy in His work of salvation; we need to weary ourselves in that service to bring His children to a knowledge of their Savior and offer them the opportunity to find relief from the ups and downs of irony found in this telestial world. If we seek for telestial rewards found in wealth, position, or acclamation, we soon find these to be fleeting and unpredictable. Our mortal life is filled with such insincerities. Jeremiah asked, concerning the ironies in life, *"Righteous art thou, O LORD, when I plead with thee: yet would I reason the cause with thee: wherefore doth the way of the wicked prosper? wherefore are all they at ease that deal very treacherously?"* (Jeremiah 12:1, Revised English Translation). We find this paradox resolved in Christ as we seek to be one with Him, which is different than learning through His Spirit. We can always learn from the Holy Ghost as we acquire the gift of faith, but to be one with Him requires a virtuous soul and a love of the Savior that becomes our motive to be like Him. The paradox of Jeremiah will not be resolved, however, as Jeremiah discovered, if our motives to serve Him are those that serve the self and not the soul.

WHY WE NEED THE RIGHT MOTIVE

While on my mission, my first experience with other's centered service, I came to know Him and learned to trust Him. As I soon discovered the fact that He is in charge, I also began to realize that it is on Him we need to focus our service, and it is to Him that we owe everything. The following story illustrates why it is so important to tend to the matters of the soul. As this wrenching event in my life will illustrate, motive in His service must be everything.

When I returned from my mission many years ago, the freeways in Salt Lake City were just being completed. The city was growing and once again, as I gained my bearings being home, I began to work for a retail-clothing store selling men's clothes and furnishings. It was there that I found a new and wonderful friend, a young man with whom I shared many interests. He was one year older than I and had served his mission in Denmark. His mission adjoined mine in Northern Germany. He sang with the Mormon Tabernacle Choir, was full of life, and because he had learned to overcome great obstacles in life, was an excellent example to me.

One day in August, on the spur-of-the-moment, we decided to go fishing after work. I was the priests' quorum advisor and the boys of my quorum had left earlier that Friday with our bishop to go into the mountains for an overnight fishing trip. We finished our shift at work at 9:00 p.m. and began to prepare to leave the Salt Lake Valley in order to meet the boys in camp. We met at my friend's home where I started to unload my gear into his Ford Mustang. It was a green car, a convertible, and very stylish. We always went in his car as mine was new, but being a Volkswagen Beetle, it was practical but not too "sexy." My friend suddenly said, "We always take my car, let's take yours." This was fine with me and we loaded our fishing gear into the front of my car and departed to the canyons. We also procured some food for our trip, things such as sunflower seeds and a few soft drinks, and as always, we brought music.

As we began to move up the canyon toward Park City, my car labored as it attempted to clear the summit. We were in fine voice, singing and laughing and very much looking forward to our Saturday in the mountains catching trout. As the car passed over the summit, it began to pick up speed. Very soon, we had reached the speed limit of 70 mph. It was then that I noticed a camper stopped on the side of the road. Since we were anxious to reach our destination, I paid it little heed. As I went to pass the camper, suddenly a horse leaped into my lane of traffic! I could not stop, and just as suddenly, we struck the horse with overpowering force. There was almost no time to apply the brakes. Because this was the case, there was an awful sound of shattering glass and the unmistakable horrific noise that accompanies metal as it collapses in on itself. It was over in seconds, but in my mind's eye, I will always remember a power that seemed to come over me and protect me from the most serious and life-threatening injuries that were likewise upon us. The small Volkswagen left the freeway and careened through a barbed-wire fence; it came to rest in a farmer's field.

My face was cut quite badly and there was a throbbing pain in my back, but I was conscious. I was then confronted with an overwhelming silence as the consequences of that event began to distil upon me. My friend was lying in my lap seriously injured. I felt paralyzed and could not move. I then heard someone calling from the highway, "Is anyone alive down there?" I was able to shout back that we were both alive, but we needed help. It wasn't too long before the police were cutting us out of the totaled car and placing us into the ambulance. My friend was still unconscious and his labored breathing led me to believe that his condition was grave; his face was swollen, but remarkably, he seemed to be at peace.

I was covered in his blood and my heart began to cry out in futile and hopeless longing, "Lord, where art Thou? Why did this just happen?" And, "Please, O Lord, bless my friend who is one of the purest men I have ever met!" Surely his bright countenance was yet needed to bless the lives of the rest of us. It was not long before the ambulance pulled into the emergency area of the University Hospital. We were separated and placed in different examining rooms. I could see my friend, his face swollen, his eyes deeply sunken, and once again, I screamed out in silence, "Help him, O Lord, is this not just a bad dream?" As the doctor began to examine me, the staff pulled closed the curtain between us and while I was aware of the intense activity that surrounded my friend, the fevered pitch of activity, I began to despair for his life.

After I was stabilized, another doctor entered my area of the emergency room. "How is my friend?" I inquired with a terrible sense of anticipation. "Son," he said, "Your friend will not last the night." I collapsed into deep despair and my thoughts suddenly focused on my Savior, knowing that I needed to trust in Him more than ever. I wanted so desperately for my friend to be made well so that we could once again continue in our association; I suddenly began to long for us to be returned to that time, a time that had just violently and unexpectedly changed, when we could again enjoy a deep and meaningful friendship. The Lord had spoken and my deep desire for healing was not to be. In my extremis, I once again cried out, but this time my prayers were not silent ones. "Precious Savior, I have learned to put my trust in Thee, my Lord, please, please help my friend and bring some comfort to him and also to me!"

As I was taken to my hospital room, and my friend was still in the emergency room, I will never forget that this would be the last time I would see him alive. I then began to realize more than ever, that not only was the Lord in charge, but more specifically, in these times especially, no offering of obedience, no efforts on my part would mold His will to mine. It was a time for me to understand the elegance of His grace and focus on His great gift of deliverance from death and sin, without any reference to my works. As I then began to accept His almighty will, His ultimate power over life and death, I also began to recognize that the feeling of protection I had felt as the accident was happening was sent by the Lord so that His will would be accomplished.

It was, however, in this time of trial that the Atonement had been fashioned and it was only under these telestial conditions that we could be born again into eternal life. Without suffering, there would be no rebirth! I was called back, to bring once again into my memory, all those doors I had knocked, all the lessons I had taught and all the time I had spent in His service—it all began to overwhelm me. In a real and poignant way, I knew that the very core of the message I had so labored to bring to the people of Germany was centered in the knowledge that the Savior had died for all those men, women and children; He had died for all those whom I had tried so hard to teach. The absolute reality of His Atonement descended upon me and this knowledge sank deep into my soul. The prescient relevance of the Atonement of Jesus Christ was at that very moment etched deeply into my soul.

My friend's parents flew down from Seattle where they recently had made their home, and they made it to the hospital before he died. They were with him and watched him take his last breath. He died at 10:00 a.m. on the very Saturday we had hoped to spend some carefree moments with the priests' quorum. I was devastated, and began to blame myself because I was driving the car. This was indeed a great irony of life; both of us were living as we should, my friend was a dynamic man, one with great abilities, and yet was struck down in the flower of his youth. As I began to embrace these events, I had no other recourse but to rely solely on the Lord.

A new reality began to dawn on me; I started to realize that even if one of them had escaped His sacrifice, if even one of them had "slipped through the cracks," that He would return again to this earth and do it all over again, even if just one had been missed. The suffering I was now feeling at the loss of a dear friend was exactly how He would feel if any were left out, even by mistake. I knew that this had been such a terrible accident, a mistake without any intent, but the consequences were devastating. I also knew that under these extreme conditions, I felt that the will of God had been accomplished and it was not for me to know why this was so. I began to truly know how precious each soul is to Him who bought us all with His precious blood. And although I had no idea that this experience would prepare me for an even greater loss in the future, the death of my wife and sweetheart, I realized in my youth that motive is everything. I knew that the gospel was more than behavior modification; it was in fact the covenant path that leads to eternal life!

How would I have felt if I had served a mission to please others? How would I have felt if my motive for service was to be rewarded by my father giving me a new car? How could I have coped with this tragedy if I had served so that I would "earn" blessings of an education, a better job, or of any worldly reward? My mission had taught me that motive is everything and with the correct motive, the Lord is able to take these kinds of tragedies into His hands and magnify our souls. When we

> **With the correct motive, the Lord is able to take these kinds of tragedies into His hands and magnify our souls**

learn to love and serve Him for the same reasons that He served us, we learn why He died for us. This then enables us to receive His image in our countenances. When we have the right motive, He can then make us better vessels to receive His truth and know of His love for all mankind. As we come to love the Lord more deeply—the truly correct motive—we see the need for repentance and the need for life's tutorials that always accompany us on life's journey. These tutorials often come as trials complete with the refining fire of suffering. The doctrines of the restoration now become invaluable in coping with the kind of pain I felt at my friend's passing. These doctrines truly did provide the "balm of Gilead" described in ancient times to heal the suffering soul.

By understanding my relationship with Him through the manner of His suffering for me, I also came to understand that such a relationship was not accomplished through casual prayer or by undertaking several programmatic steps. In such a way, we often substitute conformity for true and sighted obedience. I had learned in the mission field that motive is everything, and without an understanding of doing the right things for the right reasons, such a course would have led me into a dead end where my feelings of inadequacy, guilt, and remorse could not be healed. It was through the grace of our Lord Jesus Christ and His tender care and keeping, driven by my knowledge of the truthfulness of His gospel, that I was indeed on that very road foretold by the poet, Robert Frost, "...and I—I took the one less traveled by, and that has made all the difference" ("The Road Not Taken." *Poems of Robert Frost,* page 105).

I would have never obtained this knowledge had I not learned in the mission field to communicate with Him; had I not learned that true obedience was more than conformity and that for any obedience to be valuable, I had to be obedient for the right reasons, and first in line of those reasons was faith. Paul further taught us in Hebrews 11:6, *"But without faith it is impossible to please him; for he that cometh to God must believe that he is, and that he is a rewarder of them that diligently seek him."* Those reasons did not include being obedient to earn a reward. If we are obedient just so we obtain rewards, we are obedient so that we "get" something. This is only a simulation of faith, not real faith at all. If my motive had been to earn rewards, even at this time, my faith would have failed. My mission was only one kind of service we do as young disciples; in all venues of service, we need real faith to accomplish the work of the Lord.

My accident was over forty-five years ago and throughout my life, the Lord has seen fit to allow me to pass through even more unenviable trials—the kind through which faith is deeply tried—the trial that comes with the loss of a spouse. I am so very grateful that I learned in the mission field that motive is everything and with that knowledge, the melancholy that comes with separation either from a good friend or from one's eternal companion is swallowed up in the peace that comes from the Savior's presence in our lives. In fact, I was grateful that the Savior was both the subject as well as the object of my worship; He was the author and the finisher of my faith, like Paul explained in Hebrews 12:2. He said, *"Looking unto Jesus the author and finisher of our faith; who for the joy that was set before him endured the cross..."*

THE RIGHT MOTIVE

I had come to realize through the tragic accident discussed

above the breadth and depth of the Savior's love. With the recognition of the reality that the Savior endured the passion of His sacrifice with joy for the greater purpose, it became clear to me that I too needed to gain greater faith so that I could recognize that He endured the cross in an intimate way, for me. I needed to view Him as the author and finisher of my salvation, for His works are the only works that make this possible. I was all too happy to make Him the object of my faith, but the subject? It became clearer and clearer that as the author and finisher of my faith, He expected me to recognize His hand in these events and trust Him. Truly the Psalmist had it right when he wrote in Psalms 144:15, *"Blessed are the people to whom such blessings fall! Blessed are the people whose God is the LORD"* (English Standard Version). In order so to do—in order to be able to recognize these events as He saw them—I needed to appreciate very intimately the key element involved here, and that element was faith in the Lord Jesus Christ.

It was vital that I should come to realize that knowing His will was the primary key that would make sense of this otherwise senseless event. To comprehend His will was the key, so that I could be able to respond properly to the circumstance in which I now found myself. The key to unlock His will was to obtain a greater faith, and for that, I needed a broken heart and a contrite spirit; these are the elements of true faith. In order to do that, I knew that my response to these events was to be found in the precious knowledge that my motive for receiving that understanding was pure. With a pure motive, my

> **The key to unlock His will was to obtain a greater faith**

faith would increase. Without the correct motive, I could wallow in my grief and feign incomprehension.

I could be satiated with platitudes of general understanding and if my knowledge of His sacrifice remained vague, I would have truly become soured by not knowing the true meaning of an intimate Atonement. This all-consuming reality of a personal tragedy being embraced in an intimate Atonement was then transpiring before my very eyes. We are here not only to accept Him and His gospel, but we are here to proclaim by our very lives that He is our Sovereign, that it is His image that needs urgently to be engraved in our countenances. This is how we make Him the author of our faith, but He cannot be the finisher of this faith if we allow these occurrences not to be undergirded by impure motives. We can find no relief or comfort in these situations if our motives are self-interested. There is no relief for the pain I felt at that time outside the Atonement of the Savior and the acceptance of His will concerning the life and death of my dear friend.

This relief was to be found in Him. I had been home from my mission only eighteen months when this tragedy occurred; it was at that pressing time, as I lay in my hospital bed, that I began to be filled with the Holy Ghost. It was then that I began to seek after that same justification and His acceptance, the same witness that I had received at the end of my mission, the approbation of the Holy Ghost that the Lord accepted my weak efforts, and now in this tragedy, that He would direct my steps in the coming difficult days ahead. I began to be overwhelmed with gratitude for the example of my friend's life. It was then that the deep significance of sacrifice for the Lord's cause became supremely relevant. I began to be filled with the knowledge of how He feels about the human family as He looks upon the fallen condition that telestial living has brought upon all of us.

Through these difficult experiences, I have learned how to worship Him and I have come to know Him. The reality of His being has been a constant source of comfort to me even in times of repentance, which we all need, and in times of difficulty and of sacrifice. He is always true and faithful in every detail; it always comes back to Christ. His image stands as a beacon to us because He is the subject of our faith, the object of our worship. In those difficult days so long ago, I found an overwhelming need for faith. I needed to find assurance in the truth that His gospel had been restored through Joseph Smith, and such assurance was not available through empirical proofs or scientific reasoning. Medicine held no answers to my questions as to why this had happened. I found comfort and relief in the knowledge that Christ is at the helm. This witness provided an unwavering sense of peace in those very days of extremis.

THE WIDER AND DEEPER VIEW OF LIFE

We have identified the correct single motive for all service as disciples of Christ. However, there are other subordinate reasons for service. These, along with our primary motive of loving the Savior, will establish a correct framework for service as a disciple; it is the correct motive for caring for the sick and afflicted, as well as the correct motive for becoming married and providing for children. To uncover these reasons we must begin by asserting that our additional motives for service must be viewed with an eye that seeks the health of the soul and not of the self. It is the life of the soul that matters when we are seeking additional motives for becoming young disciples of the Savior. This actuality undergirds the primary focus of this discussion that motive is everything. Making the decision to begin a lifetime of service is a decision that should not be taken lightly.

When confronted with the reality of spiritual service and the overwhelming expectations this decision places on those who hold themselves up as disciples of Christ, we see a great array of reasons offered to the potential young disciple to induce his or her service. With so many ways to serve Him, even in the mission fields of the Church or at countless other places where young disciples are needed, each brings with him or her varied spiritual, economic, social, and educational backgrounds. So we must ask a fundamental question: Why do we choose to serve? The correct answer to this question is grounded in our motives to serve and will invariably lay the foundation for every young disciple's approach to be made ready for service.

Further, since motive is everything, when we come to understand the importance of this truth, then we will provide a framework upon which our life can be built, a life of service to God's children. We will come to better understand the mission of the sons of Mosiah and their desire to spend their entire lives, if necessary, among the Lamanites. They were prepared to remain among the Lamanites so that they might bring them the glorious knowledge of Jesus Christ and the reality of His atoning sacrifice (Alma 17:23). The joy that this thought brought to them pleased the Lord. He in turn inspired them as well as empowered them to bring His will to pass.

This correct motive provides the young disciple with an orientation and purpose that will undergird his or her preparation for any setting in which they may find themselves. As we embrace this correct motive, we find it essential to learn the doctrines of the restoration, for they illuminate the Lord's intentions regarding Himself. These doctrines include a true understanding of repentance, the absolute need for a valid baptism, as well as the doctrines of justification and sanctification. Understanding them brings us a wider and deeper view of life. Such an understanding then allows the young disciple to experience a richness in his or her service that is not possible without knowing these things.

These doctrines are the very ones the great disciples of Christ found in the Book of Mormon and the New Testament. They felt compelled, because they had been redeemed by the Savior's blood, to declare this good news to all who needed it. They knew truly that our Savior was "the Way, the Truth and the Life" for all mankind. Because these men loved the Savior and because they understood His doctrine, they were made powerful witnesses. Understanding this provides us strength when times are tough. Knowledge of these basic doctrines grounds us as young disciples in ways that allow the Spirit to build a valid and long-lasting testimony in the heart and soul of all who desire to be disciples of the Savior.

Correct motive teaches each of us to understand that the doctrines of the gospel of Jesus Christ are life-giving and that the pursuit of doctrinal knowledge provides a life-long source of certain knowledge. This then allows young servants of the Lord to be endowed with pure motives and to be filled with peace and certitude regarding their decision to serve the Lord in any situation whether at school, at work, or as a full-time missionary. As knowledge of these doctrines of the kingdom distils upon every young disciple, they are filled with vision;

they also find joy and begin to realize an eternal hope in Christ. This hope grows into an everlasting relationship with the Master as they are guided by correct motives. They are better prepared to face the rigors of discipleship, the consequence of which touch every young man or young woman as they stretch themselves in the Lord's service.

It must be made very clear to the reader that service in the Lord's cause is not about the servant and what he or she can receive from it. As we come to feed our soul and not our self, we note the nature of the food for the soul is different from the food for the self. We find self-interest as the motive for feeding the self, but Christ-centered service is the motive for feeding the soul. Appropriately then, service rendered by true young disciples of Christ is about the Lord and His work. In that light, we must come to know what He wants us to do to share His gospel and become prepared to receive His great gifts of salvation and exaltation. All servants of the Lord need to realize that their service is not about themselves, it is about those for whom Christ died. This is what Elder Boyd K. Packer has taught us with respect to missionary work, but also applies to all forms of Christ-centered service:

> The first great lesson is that this is not your mission—it is the Lord's mission. I know that we say 'I am going on my mission,' but it is not my mission, it is His mission...You will find through prayer, hard work, diligent study, and through the difficulties and disappointments you face that it is the Lord's mission. You will come to know that. ("What Every Missionary Should Know," Address given at Mission President's Seminar, June 26, 2002, page 2).

By focusing on our Savior's love for Heavenly Father's children, we overcome the natural desire to focus on ourselves; we find joy and peace in this ultimate act of service on behalf of our Father's children. Our priorities are re-ordered and our souls develop the ability to acquire truth from that ultimate source of all truth, the Holy Ghost. Correct preparation to receive new knowledge, gained through the nurture and ministry of the Holy Ghost, is vital so that an undertaking to become a disciple of Christ will lead us to the gateway gift of discipleship: faith. This kind of faith, which is far beyond mere belief, will be required in the difficult and secular days that we all know lie ahead. To be able to accomplish this great task, we must find the correct motive for service, and then our efforts at preparation will find the most fruitful results.

The Lord will help all who seek to serve Him in the best possible way, but it is only when correct motive precedes preparation that the Lord is able to help us develop great faith even by study and by prayer. We must also realize that the work of discipleship is hard work and will require a deep and abiding commitment to our Savior and His cause to save souls. As we come to embrace the solemnity of any call to serve and prepare to embark in the service of the Lord, it is a time for deep reflection, a time for the expression of gratitude, and a time to cultivate a serious sense of commitment—a time to ponder and to pray. It is a time of joy to be cherished as one of exceptional value as we prepare to leave the comfort of our homes and embark to the university, professional work, the mission field or other service focused areas. While it is a time for great joy, it is not a time for needless frivolity; preparation awaits us! Why is this important? As Elder M. Russell Ballard said:

When we are anchored to the great blessing of the Savior's life and Atonement, when our hearts are filled with gratitude to Him, we want to share our knowledge. And when we have our own internal knowledge of the doctrine, so deep and so strong, then we know that we can explain the gospel to anybody, anywhere, at any time and under any circumstances. That confidence comes from knowledge ("Missionary Work," address given at the University of Utah, Institute of Religion, October 15, 2006).

QUESTIONS ABOUT THE LESSON

01
Why is motive everything?

02
Why do we choose to serve?

03
How do we unlock His will and obtain greater faith?

04
How does true obedience follow faith?

05
Why are matters of the soul more important than matters of the self?

02

COMMUNICATING WITH THE SAVIOR

As we seek to make the decision to serve, we have learned that motive is everything and that the correct motive must be anchored to our Savior's love. This means service that is approved by our Savior—we must learn to listen to Him. Only in this way will our obedience increase our faith. As we come to love Him, our gratitude for His Atonement intensifies. It is now equally important that we learn to recognize how the Lord speaks to us and how we identify His answers. In other words, if we cannot communicate with our Savior, we cannot listen to Him. If we cannot hear His voice, how then do we make our service relevant? For if our desire to serve Him is not framed by His voice, then such service is not relevant. It will then be undertaken without any real purpose and the spiritual abilities that we might have obtained will not be found in us in any abundance. If our service is not approved by the Spirit, even with good works, it will be unfulfilling.

We see why this is so important when we consider the following poem by Myra Brooks Welch, "The Touch of the Master's Hand" (*The Gospel Messenger*, Brethren Press, 26 February 1921):

> 'Twas battered and scarred, and the auctioneer
> Thought it scarcely worth his while
> To waste much time on the old violin,
> But held it up with a smile:
> "What am I bidden, good folks," he cried,
> "Who'll start the bidding for me?"
> "A dollar, a dollar"; then, "Two!" "Only two?
> Two dollars, and who'll make it three?
> Three dollars, once; three dollars, twice;
> Going for three—" But no,
> From the room, far back, a gray-haired man
> Came forward and picked up the bow;
>
> Then, wiping the dust from the old violin,
> And tightening the loose strings,
> He played a melody pure and sweet
> As a caroling angel sings.
>
> The music ceased, and the auctioneer,
> With a voice that was quiet and low,
> Said, "What am I bid for the old violin?"
> And he held it up with the bow.
> "A thousand dollars, and who'll make it two?
> Two thousand! And who'll make it three?
>
> Three thousand, once, three thousand, twice,
> And going, and gone!" said he.

The people cheered, but some of them cried,
"We do not quite understand
What changed its worth." Swift came the reply:
"The touch of a master's hand."

And many a man with life out of tune,
And battered and scarred with sin,
Is auctioned cheap to the thoughtless crowd,
Much like the old violin.
A "mess of pottage," a glass of wine,
A game—and he travels on.

He's "going" once, and "going" twice,
He's "going" and almost "gone."
But the Master comes, and the foolish crowd
Never can quite understand
The worth of a soul and the change that's wrought
By the touch of the Master's hand.

This poem is quite an illustration of the difference the touch of the Master's hand will make in our lives. Our service to Christ is made relevant only when our service is touched by the Master's hand. He cannot touch us if we cannot communicate with Him. He touches our lives as we seek to be born again. Sometimes being born again is described as a process. It is, however, not really a process as much as it is a series of events that change our heart, and as these events commence, we are able to hear His voice. As these events of spiritual rebirth begin to unfold in our lives, it must be clear to all that they do not occur unless we can communicate with our Savior. It is also clear that the old man who made such beautiful music had been touched by the hand of the Master; he was one that knew the worth of a soul and he was one that knew that through the Master's touch, a soul was beautifully changed. He had learned to listen to the Savior's voice and then, he responded. The old man now knew the worth of souls was great in the eyes of God.

This is what we seek when we strive to communicate with our Savior: we seek His touch in our hearts, His blessing of our soul, and His approval of our efforts. It is this approval, the one that comes through being justified by the Spirit, that we cannot find if we do not truly learn to communicate with Him. He answers our pleas for justification through the Holy Ghost. If we cannot find Him through prayer, we are uncertain of our way and find ourselves "flying blind" on the path of life, or we lack vision as to why we keep the commandments. If this happens, typically we conform to the law without the Spirit; this is why Paul taught us, *"And such trust have we through Christ to God-ward: Not that we are sufficient of ourselves to think any thing as of ourselves; but our sufficiency is of God; Who also hath made us able ministers of the new testament; not of the letter, but of the spirit: for the letter killeth, but the spirit giveth life"* (2 Corinthians 3:4–6). Accordingly, we must seek His face through our faith and let Him give life to our obedience.

FINDING RELEVANCE IN THE GOSPEL

As we pursue Him, we seek His touch. It is in His touch that we find relevance in His service. Relevance begins when we can start to answer King Benjamin's question, found in Mosiah 5:13, *"For how knoweth a man the master whom he has not served, and who is a stranger unto him, and is far from the thoughts and intents of his heart?"* As we are able to be born again and can then see the kingdom of God (John 3:3), we will desire above all not only to enter His Kingdom, but to grow our love for Him. Our greatest desire will be found in pleasing Him. In short, we will want to know Him as He is and thereby, not only make the music of salvation, but also find rest in such songs of redeeming love. We read in Alma 5:26, *"And now behold, I say unto you, my brethren, if ye have experienced a change of heart, and if ye have felt to sing the song of redeeming love, I would ask, can ye feel so now?"*

We sing this song of redeeming love, as we are able to communicate effectively with Him. We find, as we sing these hymns of praise to Him, that His image begins to be engraved upon our countenance and we are justified before Him as we listen in faith and do the things He tells us. We become a new creature, born of His Spirit; we become a new man or a new woman, with an eye single to Him and His cause. As we begin to find acute relevance in the gospel of Jesus Christ, we find that our entire lives will need to reflect His goodness and mercy. We will then be able to devote time to meditation, to reflection and pondering, for in these kinds of self-evident action is our ability to listen to the Lord enhanced.

As we have attended our church meetings, we have received many lessons on how to recognize the Spirit in our lives. Often, these lessons did not receive the attention they deserved largely because we were young and concerned with growing up. Parents have been diligent in teaching their children about how the Spirit works and how we receive answers to our prayers, but in our youth, we have at times been casual about prayer, and indifferent about receiving answers from our Heavenly Father. We have often confused an emotional expression or outburst with the answers provided by the Holy Ghost. This usually happens when we experience new sensations as we grow to love our friends, experience the growth of knowledge in secular fields, or when we seek higher education.

When the time comes to confront the decision to serve a mission, the need for real spiritual answers becomes acute. No longer can emotion serve as a substitute for communication from the Savior; no longer can we rely on "steps of conformity" and expect to receive any answer that makes sense to our own particular circumstances. We need to know for ourselves why the Lord will ask us to serve and give forth our effort, even sacrificing much in His service; even as we seek to serve in many locations and in specific ways. The true reasons are not found in matters of the self. Of course such service in the mission field will help us to be better workers, better students, and better husbands and wives. But, if we do not learn to listen in faith, our souls will not be changed or reborn. Our understanding of the touch of the Master's hand will be shallow and our deep conversion to His cause will languish, as our focus will remain on things of the self and not the soul-changing events that pertain to being born again. This is what is meant by finding our true sense of being. Our intent for service will be real and our willingness to serve Him will become our single objective.

> **We need to know for ourselves why the Lord will ask us to serve**

COMMUNICATING WITH REAL INTENT

One day, when a particular young man was seeking answers, he told his bishop that he had not received an answer to his prayer concerning missionary service. This is a common problem when considering any kind of service in the Lord's kingdom. The bishop told him just to decide to go on his mission and that then he would discover he had made the right choice. This is an unfortunate response because missionary service, like all service in the Lord's cause requires us to feed our soul so that we can serve others. His stake president recognized the error and told the young man that, as his stake president, he would not let the young man serve until he had received an answer to his prayer concerning his desire for missionary service. This same advice holds for any other service to which the Lord may inspire a young disciple. He further explained that now was the time for him to learn how answers come. Once the young man had learned this lesson, he could then serve his mission with distinction and purpose and he would be prepared for all service in the Lord's kingdom.

The stake president was wise, for when this young man actually learned how to communicate with the Lord, his prayer was answered and he served a very capable mission in a faraway land where the people were deeply steeped in tradition. In other words, his sense of being—meaning his sense of his own spiritual existence—was now connected to God and not confused with the self. This was important because his mission was in a difficult place and his sense of being was an overriding requirement; the need to communicate with the Lord was paramount. As a young disciple, we all need to learn this lesson early for it will serve us for the rest of our lives.

In his quest for both answers and relevance, he found that there are no secret steps involved in obtaining answers from the Lord. The scriptures provide numerous examples of how prayers are answered. We see that in order to communicate with the Lord, the one needful thing is a sense of focused desire; a sense of real intent is required to receive answers. Thus we find relevance and purpose for our inquiries. Real intent tutors the soul as it seeks to be re-ordered along the lines of the Savior's priorities. We have been asked to pray for a witness concerning the Book of Mormon in Moroni 10:4, *"And when ye shall receive these things, I would exhort you that ye would ask God, the Eternal Father, in the name of Christ, if these things are not true; and if ye shall ask with a sincere heart, with real intent, having faith in Christ, he will manifest the truth of it unto you, by the power of the Holy Ghost."*

We must be willing to leave our comfort zone and truly seek after His will, not ours. This is yet another reason why our motive is so important; we must have the correct motive in order to receive an answer to our prayers and in that way, the answers are relevant. We learn from Moroni's words anew: motive is everything. And in this case, our motive must be centered in our Savior and our desire to know from Him directly, through the power of the Holy Ghost, the answer to our prayer. It is then that our search becomes truly relevant. In other words, Moroni teaches us that we must have faith in Christ and not substitute this faith, which comes from our desire for real intent, by undertaking any shortcuts.

> **We must be willing to leave our comfort zone and truly seek after His will, not ours**

These diversions often come when well-intentioned people want us to seek for behavior modification steps in lieu of the hard work required to refine our intent and make it real. And while our behavior is changed when we undertake such a course, often for the good, if our hearts are not changed, our intent becomes confused and answers to our prayers are not forthcoming or are uncertain. Real intent is a matter of the heart and not a matter of self-improvement. If we make it such then our prayers go unanswered and we remain frustrated. It is only when we learn to subordinate our will to His—by re-ordering our priorities to reflect His priorities—that we will find the courage to ask with real intent. This is a matter of faith and not of works; it is the heart and the soul that seek for answers from the Holy Ghost, not the self.

In light of Moroni's words, we learn that the terms "willing" and "real intent" are irretrievably linked. As they are coupled together, the relevance of prayer is self-evident. In our world of scientific discovery, this is not always easily recognized, as science has no way of measuring intent or willingness. These cannot be determined by sight, sound, touch, or any of our senses, and because of this, prayer is often viewed as irrelevant. We recognized in Welch's poem that the touch of the Master did not come as result of a physical touching; it came as the soul and heart of the old man were touched by the music of the Spirit. The touch of the Master's hand caused the old man's soul to be re-ordered. Likewise, our lives may be healed by His touch. This tells us that if we seek for a rationalized answer to spiritual questions, we become frustrated, because in the realm where answers are discovered by scientific experimentation, we find such a field to be barren and unfulfilling with respect to the Spirit. The answers we seek are not found in science; they are, however, found in faith.

FINDING ANSWERS THROUGH FAITH

We will find our answers as we come to understand how to focus our faith so that it will create within us real intent, and with that focus, we will also uncover a proper willingness to act on our answer. For many, this will be a new experience, as normally when we pray in our youth, we are seeking to earn blessings. This is exactly the wrong motive when it comes to finding answers to our prayers concerning our service be it at school, work or as a full-time missionary. We have already learned that the correct motive is anchored in Christ and in His will, not ours. This must become a prelude in approaching Him; it must be that the reasons for our pending service correspond to the will of God and not our will. How do we find the right motive so that our intent will be real and our willingness to serve will be centered in Christ and not in ourselves? In connection with that question, there is a companion question: "How do we learn to suppress our will so that our willingness to find an answer is bound together with our love of the Savior?"

So often in our modern world—with electronic devices and other gadgets that make our lives easier and when we have so many programs that are designed to help us with our work—we become complacent. We no longer place enough emphasis on the age-old method of gaining answers to our prayers. What we are seeking as we begin to make the decision to serve for the right reasons is what Nicodemus desired when he approached the Savior, as recorded in John 3:1–2, *"There was a man of the Pharisees, named Nicodemus, a ruler of the Jews: The same came to Jesus by night, and said unto him, Rabbi, we know that thou art a teacher come from God: for no man can do these miracles that thou doest, except God be with him."* Like most of us who seek an answer from God, we too understand intellectually, as did Nicodemus, that Jesus must come from God.

Nicodemus, by approaching the Savior in this manner, demonstrated that he had at least some rudimentary faith. This is often the case with those who seek an answer with respect to serving a mission. The answer Nicodemus received amplified his faith and set him in a new direction, away from the sightless obedience of the Pharisees. He was instructed that he must be born again to both see and enter the kingdom of God. It is the goal of every Latter-day Saint to follow in Nicodemus' footsteps and seek those events that are designated as events of spiritual rebirth. These events begin when we accept the Savior and His work as being superior to our work. Being born again will then govern the way we are obedient to His commandments and how we seek to magnify our service. No longer will we seek to earn our blessings, but instead, because our motive is right, we will seek to receive His blessings because we trust Him. We are obedient to Him so that we may be like Him and thus more able to serve Him and receive the blessings He has promised for that service

Since the decision at hand revolves around becoming a true disciple, we begin to realize that He is the consummate example of all service designed to bring souls to Him. In order then to enter His service, we must receive an answer from Him through the Holy Ghost, as He promised. Thus, it is assumed that this kind of a decision is being undertaken by those who already have embraced His message through baptism, and now wish to bring this good news to others.

QUESTIONS ABOUT THE LESSON

01
What is the "touch of the Master's hand," and how does it change lives?

02
Why does the Gospel need to be relevant?

03
How do we create real intent and become truly willing to receive the Spirit?

04
How can we keep the lines of communication open with God and what do we do if we are not getting an answer?

05
Why is it necessary to recognize the Spirit in faith and how do we best identify the Spirit in our lives?

03

BEING BORN AGAIN

The scriptures make reference to the need to be born again. What does that mean? In Lesson Two, we noted that Nicodemus exhibited at least a rudimentary faith when he approached the Savior seeking an answer as to how he performed the miracles that all had witnessed. Nicodemus' example illustrates what happens every day when men and women seek after knowledge of things they do not understand. This is the underlying question asked in Welch's poem, "The Touch of the Master's Hand" also found in the prior lesson. There, the old violinist knew of the Master's touch and it affected his entire life and the lives of those with whom he had come in contact. The conversation that the poet had with us, illustrated in that poem, can now be expanded to embrace Nicodemus' question as well.

One such example from the world of science will illustrate how these kinds of conversations lead us to uncover the need to be born again. This example is found in the life of Albert Einstein (*Einstein's Cosmos: How Albert Einstein's Vision*

Transformed Our Understanding of Space and Time, pages 59–90). It will illustrate how God's knowledge of things as they really are can be obtained. Einstein had talked for hours with many scientists about the concept of Newton's laws of absolute space and time, which seemed to violate Maxwell's constancy of the speed of light. Eventually, totally exhausted, Einstein announced that he was finished. He could not resolve this paradox; he felt defeated. Although he was depressed and felt empty, he continued to think about the paradox as he returned home one evening in Zurich, Switzerland. His mind turned in particular to a time he was similarly on a streetcar in Bern, a time when he was looking back at the famous clock tower at city-center.

He imagined what would happen if his streetcar raced away from the clock tower at the speed of light. He quickly realized that the clock would appear stopped since light could then not catch up to the streetcar! But time within the streetcar itself would pass normally. Then it suddenly hit him—the key to the complete paradox was now before him. He said, "A storm broke loose in my mind!" It was a revelation of being able to see; it was not a mathematical breakthrough but instead he was able to see something that had been there all the time but because we are trapped in a world of phenomena, it had been hidden from him. Einstein now knew the answer was simple and elegant: time can beat at different rates throughout the universe, depending on how fast one moved.

This revelation happened because Einstein turned his soul to the light found outside his being. It was an "ah-hah." For the next six weeks, he furiously worked out every mathematical detail of this brilliant insight. This "ah-hah" led to a paper that is arguably one of the most important scientific papers of all time: $E=mc^2$, which became the mathematical expression of a concept that came to Einstein because he had been born again scientifically. He had turned his soul to the enlightened source of all light—to God—because he was unable to use the tools he then possessed to resolve the paradox that lay before him. It is clear that unless Einstein was able to access a source unknown to him, the paradox would have never been resolved and the simple but profound mathematical expression of his vision would have not been realized.

So it is with us. Charles Taylor, a modern-day ethics philosopher, has said we must "[turn] the whole soul from darkness to brightness of true being" (*Sources of the Self,* page 123). The context of such a statement is this: just as the eye cannot exercise its function of seeing unless there is a reality there and it is properly illuminated, so reason cannot realize its proper function until we are turned toward real being, a being that is illuminated by God. If we are only illuminated by facts not set in this context, we remain blind. This is what being born again accomplishes; it turns our attention from matters of the self to matters of the soul. Even in matters of science and philosophy, these scholars recognize the need to see beyond themselves.

> **We must turn the whole soul from darkness to brightness of true being.**

This was well known by our Lord, and we discover that He does understand this in the way He answered Nicodemus. He shows us how to turn our whole souls from darkness to light when he instructed Nicodemus that he must be born again to see the kingdom of God. That we all must be born again is a matter discussed in all of our scriptures, and as disciples, we must be about this business of being born again. It is a life-long project that takes us along the path less traveled, as we discovered in Lesson One; it is the path the poet identified as the path "wanting wear," and it is the path that will make all the difference in our lives (see again, "The Road Not Taken." *Poems of Robert Frost*, page 105).

THE JOURNEY BEGINS WITH PRAYER

As we uncover the connection between finding the real intent within us and then combining this intent with our willingness to come to know the Savior and feel of His love, we arrive at a great truth: by linking the events of real intent and focused willingness toward the Savior, as we discovered above, we find that the events which then begin to unfold are new and refreshing. These new manifestations pertain to the heart, and as they commence, we begin to experience what the Savior calls being born again. These happenings are dynamic and exhilarating, just as Nicodemus found them to be. We read in John 3:3, "*Jesus answered and said unto him, Verily, verily, I say unto thee, Except a man be born again, he cannot see the kingdom of God.*" When we hear this term, *born again*, we often think of born again Christians and wonder what that has to do with us. We are often confused by this term because we assume, as do they, that by simply accepting Jesus as our Savior, no other actions promoted by faith are required. This is not the case.

The fact is we all need to be born again, as the Lord explained in John 3:5, and this cannot happen without faith in the Lord Jesus Christ. Without faith, it is impossible to please

Him (see Hebrews 11:6). Moreover, to have faith we must acknowledge that salvation comes by Christ, as Lehi explained to Jacob in 2 Nephi 2:8, *"Wherefore, how great the importance to make these things known unto the inhabitants of the earth, that they may know that there is no flesh that can dwell in the presence of God, save it be through the merits, and mercy, and grace of the Holy Messiah..."* What the Savior acknowledged in Nicodemus was his faith, preliminary as it was, and what that implied in his faith was the understanding Lehi taught Jacob: it is solely the work of the Christ that saves us, not our works. It is His work that is superior and is all that is required. Our works, while important because they identify the fact that our soul has been turned to His light, only make our faith perfect.

So, when Nicodemus asked what being born again meant and *"Jesus answered, Verily, verily, I say unto thee, Except a man be born of water and of the Spirit, he cannot enter into the kingdom of God,"* He is telling Nicodemus that it is by faith we are saved. And if our faith is redemptive, it will be attended by good works so that this redemptive faith can be made perfect (see James 2:22). The Lord is making reference to a few things here. First, we cannot see the kingdom of God, meaning we cannot get answers to our prayers and see what we are to do, unless we are born again, and this is entirely within the concept of faith. Second, once we get an answer, we must be willing to act on that answer. In the case of Nicodemus, once he could see the truth by his faith, he then needed to be baptized with water and receive the gift of the Holy Ghost in order to enter the kingdom of God. So we too must be born again to both see and enter the kingdom of God, which means we need to have the correct motive, real intent, and a willingness to do what the

Lord asks of us.

BORN OF THE WATER AND THE SPIRIT

After we have been born again to see the kingdom of God, the Lord then told Nicodemus how he could enter this kingdom. As noted above, it was being born of the water and of the Spirit. If we are saved in faith by grace, why is baptism completely consistent with the concept of being saved by grace? Moreover, why is this consistent with the concept of being born again? We read in 2 Nephi 31:13, *"Wherefore, my beloved brethren, I know that if ye shall follow the Son, with full purpose of heart, acting no hypocrisy and no deception before God, but with real intent, repenting of your sins, witnessing unto the Father that ye are willing to take upon you the name of Christ, by baptism—yea, by following your Lord and your Savior down into the water, according to his word, behold, then shall ye receive the Holy Ghost; yea, then cometh the baptism of fire and of the Holy Ghost; and then can ye speak with the tongue of angels..."* Is it now clear why the Lord told Nicodemus he must be born of the water and the Spirit to enter the kingdom of God?

This is pretty basic doctrine. Baptism is essential (see Mark 16:16). Accordingly, it must be performed by one who has the authority to act in the name of the Lord. We see that the ancient apostles were given this authority by the Savior. We read in Luke 9:1, *"Then calling the Twelve together He conferred on them power and authority over all the demons and to cure diseases"* (Weymouth New Testament). It is clear that Jesus intended that those who act in His name have authority conferred upon them by Him. But what about John the Baptist, did he not act with authority and since he preceded Jesus, how did he obtain this authority? We read of the miraculous circumstances of John's birth in Luke 1:13 and 16–17, *"But the angel said to him, Do not be afraid, Zechariah, for your petition has been heard: and your wife Elizabeth will bear you a son, and you are to call his name John… Many of the descendants of Israel will he turn to the Lord their God; and he will be His forerunner in the spirit and power of Elijah, to turn fathers' hearts to the children, and cause the rebellious to walk in the wisdom of the upright, to make a people perfectly ready for the Lord"* (Weymouth New Testament).

These words were spoken by the angel Gabriel to Zachariah, John's father, as he was officiating in priesthood ordinances in the temple. Zacharias had the authority of the priesthood given to him before Gabriel visited him. This was according to the Lord's pattern of conferring authority, he received this revelation concerning the birth of his son because he was already authorized by the Levitical priesthood to receive such a vision. It was also widely known by other priesthood administrator's that he had such authority. This is what makes this testimony and that of John the Baptist binding on us. Notice that when John fulfilled his calling he knew he had the authority to call Israel to repentance. We read of John's mission in Matthew 3:3 and 6–8, *"This is he who was spoken of through the prophet Isaiah: A voice of one calling in the wilderness, Prepare the way for the Lord, make straight paths for him. Confessing their sins, they were baptized of him in the Jordan River. But when he saw many of the Pharisees and Sadducees coming to where he was baptizing, he said to them: You brood of vipers! Who warned you to flee from the coming wrath? Produce fruit in keeping with repentance"* (New International Version).

The pattern for receiving the Lord's authority to baptize is established in the New Testament: it is given to men by the passing on of keys by God Himself or more likely, through legal administrators also sanctioned by God. It is this authority to which Paul referred when he explained this method to those who embraced the new covenant. In Hebrews 5:4 and 6, *"And no one can become a high priest simply because he wants such an honor. He must be called of God for this work, just as Aaron was"* (New Living Translation). Even if we see the physical image of Christ, unless this pattern on how authority is conferred is followed, we can rest assured such a person claiming such authority, even if he or she claims to have seen the resurrected Lord, the pattern to be called of God and not of men is clear: it is accomplished in the same manner as it was when Aaron received priesthood authority. It comes by prophets and apostles who have the keys to pass this authority to others. As Paul taught, just because we want this authority, we cannot claim it unless it is conferred on us according to this pattern.

Further, it must be generally known by those in authority that such a person has this authority, as it was shown in the calling of John the Baptist. We read in Acts 8:14–16, *"Now when the apostles which were at Jerusalem heard that Samaria had received the word of God, they sent unto them Peter and John: Who, when were come down, prayed for them, that they might receive the Holy Ghost: (For as yet he was fallen upon none of them: only they were baptized in the name of the Lord Jesus.) Then laid they their hands on them, and they received the Holy Ghost."* It is through the laying on of hands by those who hold the keys and are known to hold them, that the Holy Ghost is conferred; it is the same with all priesthood ordinances.

Even though the apostles were called and ordained by the Savior Himself (see John 15:16), they still needed keys to pass on the gift of the Holy Ghost. Remember, it is the conferring of the Holy Ghost that allows us to be born of the Spirit, and it is with this authority that we must be baptized. These keys were also necessary to pass this authority to others. This is why the Lord took Peter, James and John up to the Mount of Transfiguration (see Matthew 17:1–7 and 10–13). It was there that these apostles received the keys of the priesthood and could both pass the priesthood to others and perform confirmations where the gift of the Holy Ghost was likewise conferred by the laying on of hands. This is the method the disciples used to fulfill the commandment of the Lord in Matthew 28:19–20, *"Therefore go and make disciples of all nations, baptizing them in the name of the Father and of the Son and of the Holy Spirit, and teach them to obey everything I have commanded you. And surely I am with you always, to the very end of time"* (New International Version). Because they had authority given them after this pattern, they baptized proselytes in water by immersion and then by the laying on of hands, they conferred the gift of the Holy Ghost.

This is true of the Twelve Apostles today. This pattern was followed by Joseph Smith. In 1829, he and Oliver Cowdery received the Aaronic priesthood by the laying on of hands through John the Baptist; they received the Melchizedek priesthood in the same way from Peter, James and John. Further, in the Kirtland Temple the events that happened on the Mount of Transfiguration occurred as recorded in Doctrine and Covenants 110. This is why Parley P. Pratt explained the need for such keys delivered to mankind in that same manner:

> This great and good man [Joseph Smith] was led, before his death, to call the Twelve together from time to time, and to instruct them in all things pertaining to the kingdom, ordinances, and government of God. He often observed that he was laying the foundation, but it would remain for the Twelve to complete the building. Said he, "I know not why; but for some reason I am constrained to hasten my preparations, and to confer upon the Twelve all the ordinances, keys, covenants, endowments, and sealing ordinances of the priesthood... for said he, the Lord is about to lay the burden on your shoulders and let me rest awhile... the kingdom of God will roll on, and I have now finished the work which was laid upon me, by committing to you all things for the building up of the kingdom according to the heavenly vision and the pattern shown me from heaven" ("Proclamation," *Millennial Star*, vol. 5, March 1845, page 149).

WALKING THE PATH OF HOLINESS

We have come to understand that we must have faith to see the kingdom of God, and without faith, any action is not pleasing to God (see Hebrews 11:6). So we must proceed in faith, but how? We are only at the beginning as we turn our whole soul to the light and take those first steps of baptism and confirmation. In Alma 7:19 and 23–24 we read, *"For I perceive that ye are in the path of righteousness; I perceive that ye are in the path which leads to the kingdom of God; yea, I perceive that ye are making his paths straight... And now I would that ye should be humble, and be submissive and gentle; easy to be entreated; full of patience and long-suffering; being temperate in all things; being diligent in keeping the commandments of God at all times; asking for whatsoever things ye stand in need, both spiritual and temporal; always returning thanks to God for whatsoever ye do receive. And see that ye have faith, hope, and charity, and then ye will always abound in good works."* If we do not embrace these traits and strive to change our nature from the "natural man" to the "man that is born again," our spiritual rebirth will be aborted. To change our nature, it requires heavenly intervention, such as that recorded by Alma as he was miraculously delivered from the effects of sin and of the determinism that is part of being the natural man. We read in Alma 36:17–20, *"And it came to pass that as I was thus racked with torment, while I was harrowed up by the memory of my many sins, behold, I remembered also to have heard my father prophesy unto the people concerning the coming of one Jesus Christ, a Son of God, to atone for the sins of the world. Now, as my mind caught hold upon this thought, I cried within my heart: O Jesus thou Son of God, have mercy on me, who am in the gall of bitterness... And now, behold, when I thought this, I could remember my pains no more; yea, I was harrowed up by the memory of my sins no more. And oh, what joy, and what marvelous light I did behold; yea, my soul was filled with joy as exceeding as was my pain!"*

Alma's nature was changed; he embraced faith, hope and charity and in so doing, all of his actions from then on would be governed by the faith produced by his broken and contrite heart. His obedience would be sighted and he would make the Master the subject as well as the object of his faith. No lists, no behavior-modification steps; he was born of God and the path of holiness was engaged. He was now a new being, having been born again through the Spirit of the Holy Ghost. His service was dedicated to the Savior and certainly not as a reward for "good works." We now see that the events of being born again are inseparable from those that pertain to discipleship. A true disciple seeks to both see and enter the kingdom of God. All of this begins with real intent and a correct motive as we pray for this mighty change. We will then be like the faithful Nicodemus who sought and found this path of holiness through meditation and prayer. His faith was thereby empowered.

HOW TO BE BORN AGAIN

We are not born again all at once unless the event is so singular or so miraculous as those recorded in scripture. Alma the Younger is such an example as we have shown above. Another example of such a singular event is Paul, in the New Testament. We read of Paul's conversion and the events that marked the event of his rebirth in Acts 9:3–17. We also take note that even after such a momentous experience, and the fact that Paul's soul had begun to be re-ordered by seeing the Lord in this great vision, he still needed, as stated in verse 18, to be baptized in order to enter the kingdom of God. The events of being born again do not replace the need for ordinances.

Ordinances allow us to enter the kingdom of God. Our Savior also expressed this view simply when He said, *"He that believeth and is baptized shall be saved; but he that believeth not shall be damned"* (Mark 16:16). We enter the kingdom by the water of baptism and then by confirmation, just as our Savior taught Nicodemus in John 3:5, as discussed above. The connection between the need to see the kingdom of God and entering said kingdom is enabled by baptism. This is important, for if we are not prepared to receive the ordinances of salvation; the events of being born again are aborted, because without baptism and then confirmation—the receipt of the gift of the Holy Ghost—we cannot enter the kingdom of God. As these events of being born again unfold, we will need additional ordinances—those of the temple—after we enter at the gate of baptism. We must, however, begin the events of being born again where they start, and that means we commence our spiritual rebirth with "seeing" the kingdom of God, seeking Him in faith. The events of being born again begin when we seek to find our Savior, which comes as we acknowledge our need for faith in Him. Elder Bruce R. McConkie said:

> We say that a man has to be born again, meaning that he has to die as pertaining to the unrighteous things of the world. Paul said, "Crucify the old man of sin and come forth in a newness of life" (Romans 6:6). We are born again when we die as pertaining to unrighteousness and when we live as pertaining to the things of the Spirit. But that does not happen in an instant.... As far as the generality of the members of the Church are concerned, we are born again by degrees, and we are born again to added light and added knowledge and added desires for righteousness as we keep the commandments.... I think we ought to have great hope, I think we ought to have rejoicing (*The Life Beyond,* pages 138–139).

So, how do we begin? How do we begin to "see the kingdom of God?" We will see that real intent and a willingness to receive an answer are fundamental in the following scriptural illustrations. It is clear in the scriptures that if we look at Alma the Younger or Paul, the events that lead to their being born again began with prayer. In Alma the Younger's case, it was the prayer of his father, Alma, as well as a result of many faithful people that brought these events of spiritual rebirth to pass in the life of his son. We read in Mosiah 27:14, *"And again, the angel said: Behold, the Lord hath heard the prayers of his people, and also the prayers of his servant, Alma, who is thy father; for he has prayed with much faith concerning thee that thou mightest be brought to the knowledge of the truth; therefore, for this purpose have I come to convince thee of the power and authority of God, that the prayers of his servants might be answered according to their faith."* With respect to our other example, Paul, we know that he was like Alma the Younger, an enemy to the work of God, and like Alma and the sons of Mosiah, he went about destroying the Lord's work.

Although it is not recorded, we can assume that many faithful members of Christ's church were praying for Saul of Tarsus' mission not to succeed. And in response to those prayers, the Lord rebuked Saul on the road to Damascus. But along with that rebuke, we read in Acts 9:11 of Ananias and the reason he went to visit Saul, *"And the Lord said unto him, Arise, and go into the street which is called Straight, and inquire in the house of Judas for one called Saul, of Tarsus: for, behold, he prayeth."* In the previous lesson, we learned that communication with the Savior is an absolute requirement as we uncover the need to re-order our souls; in connection with this need, we learned that the ability to listen to the Savior is likewise indispensable. To memorialize this re-ordering, Saul of Tarsus became Paul. It is with real intent, found in sacred prayer, that both the relevance of our service is developed and that our true motive for such service, the love of Christ, is found. It is in this way we experience the touch of the Master's hand and then His image begins to be engraved in our countenances. We find such desire in the hymn, "Prayer is the Soul's Sincere Desire!"

Previously, we have seen that the events that lead to being born again begin with prayer; if not our prayers, then the prayers of other faithful members who seek for our welfare. Can we not see that both Alma and Saul of Tarsus prayed with real intent? They were like many of us today, and although they had seen a vision and beheld the physical presence of the Lord, they were still in need of "seeing the kingdom of God," and wanted the Lord to answer their prayers. They were praying with real intent, and were willing to do whatever the Lord wanted, so that these prayers could be answered and the truth concerning their particular circumstances could be revealed.

SPIRITUAL REBIRTH

In both of these examples, the occasion of being born again was triggered by miraculous events. As we noted above, for most of us this does not happen—we are born again by degrees. But in every case, miraculous or not, such an event of being born again commences with prayer, sincere prayer, offered with real intent and with faith in Christ. This intent is then accompanied by a willingness to follow through when we receive an answer. These are indispensable elements that are required to begin the journey that leads to being born again. So that we can receive answers to our prayers, just as Moroni told us regarding gaining a witness of the Book of Mormon, as we seek for discipleship, our motive must be right and our intent real.

Remember, the knowledge for which we are seeking and

the life we are called to live cannot be found if we seek spiritual rebirth as a science experiment; intent and willingness cannot be measured by the senses. They are matters of the heart. So it is here we must begin, with the heart, to uncover the attributes of real intent. As we begin to pray, we seek to change our heart; it is then, as our heart changes that the events of being born again continue. We are not talking about physical birth, as that has already happened, but about spiritual birth, an event for which the heart and soul yearns. Spiritual birth commences, as Elder McConkie explained, when we "crucify the old man of sin," and seek a new life governed by righteousness. This is the path of holiness and it is never an easy one. It is often filled with challenges, pain, suffering and regrets; it is however never filled with vacillation or ulterior motives.

> **Spiritual birth commences when we "crucify the old man of sin," and seek a new life governed by righteousness**

This then is the purpose of our lives in mortality. Once the events of being born again commence, we must also realize they can be stopped; the events of rebirth can be terminated if we return again to that "old man of sin." This can also happen if we perfunctorily conform to the commandments in the hope that it will be our conformity and deeds of themselves and not the Christ alone that will save us. This is folly. On the other hand, to be filled with the Holy Ghost is one of the most sublime features of learning by the Spirit. President Dallin H. Oaks has taught us concerning being born again. He tells us that being born again happens every week:

> The Book of Mormon has many teachings about the necessity of being "born again" or "born of God" (see Mosiah 27:24-26; Alma 36:24, 26; Moses 6:59). As we understand these scriptures, our answer to whether we have been born again is clearly "yes." We are born again when we entered into a covenant relationship with our Savior by being born of water and of the Spirit and by taking upon us the name of Jesus Christ. We can renew that rebirth each Sabbath when we partake of the sacrament ("Have You Been Saved?" *Ensign,* May 1998).

So, how do we now make a successful beginning? As we have shown, any event of being born again or of receiving answers about what kind of discipleship our service will embrace begins when we kneel in prayer. Is this not the way Joseph Smith began? Joseph was seeking a new life; he was concerned about his soul and the saving of it. We may safely say, he was seeking the ability to see the kingdom of God so that his concerns regarding his soul could be healed; he was seeking a born-again experience. It was under these conditions that he turned to prayer. He did not pray so that he could found a new church. It was the concern he had for his soul that motivated his prayer (*The Papers of Joseph Smith* 1:6). He read in James 1:5, *"If any of you lack wisdom, let him ask of God, that giveth to all men liberally, and upbraideth not; and it shall be given him. But let him ask in faith, nothing wavering."* We see that the Lord is fully consistent in the scriptures when it comes to prayer.

When we pray, we must be careful not to "upbraid" the Lord. This means we must not scold or rebuke the Lord for our circumstances, nor should we feel entitled to an answer. We should expect an answer, but not feel entitled to one. If we feel entitled, we are scolding or rebuking the Lord because we have set ourselves at the center of our prayer where our needs come before His needs and the self comes before the heart. This kills real intent. We must put ourselves aside and ask the Lord for His greater good—the good of His kingdom. After all, our service is to advance His kingdom, so, it stands to reason, prayers about service in His work should focus on Him, the author of that work.

DISCOVERING HIS WILL FOCUSES FAITH

We need to focus on the events of being born again so that we will be able to ascertain His will concerning our service in His kingdom. This requires that we initiate those events that lead us to being born again; we seek for those events that will re-order our soul so that its focus is on Him, not ourselves. We must realize that as part of being born again, we need to see the kingdom of God first, and then we must re-order our priorities to reflect His interests. When we do so, we find confidence in our ability to obtain an answer to our prayers. This is what is required of us so that we might obtain His intent, the real intent for why we are seeking answers. It is with this intent that our answer can be revealed to us. In order for us to put the Lord's priorities before our main concerns, He tells us in Doctrine and Covenants 112:10, *"Be thou humble; and the Lord thy God shall lead thee by the hand, and give thee answer to thy prayers."*

Humility is not an easy trait to acquire. In our world, where we seem to have the victories of science at our very fingertips, and where we exalt success in any form above failure, it is easy for us to find success and hence hard to find humility. Because we know that humility is a desired trait, we often feign being humble so that we might be seen as someone who is humble, but in fact we are really arrogant about being humble. This is a travesty to be avoided at all costs. As we become meek, we will find that the Spirit will attend us each week as we partake of the sacrament; we will find ourselves justified by the Spirit as the promises of the sacrament prayers are realized, *"... that they may always have his Spirit to be with them. Amen"* (Doctrine and Covenants 20:77).

Everyone loves a winner and even in our church, we seem to praise those who make the most money; we love the best athlete and hope to be like him or her. We value effort, but only the effort that brings tangible success. Often, effort that seems to be squandered on inefficient pursuits is rejected as not contributing to winning. This is very unfortunate. Perhaps if we view effort in its proper context, we would see it differently. In Mark 10:15 we read, *"Verily I say unto you, Whosoever shall not receive the kingdom of God as a little child, he shall no wise enter therein"* (English Revised Version). So the first clue with respect to effort comes to us if we are able to be humble when exerting effort. In other words, what is our motive? If we are humble, like a little child, even if not successful, our efforts will be approved of the Lord. In Matthew 18:4, we find this clarification, *"Whosoever therefore shall humble himself as this little child, the same is greatest in the kingdom of heaven."*

QUESTIONS ABOUT THE LESSON

01
How are we born again?

02
How is Einstein's example relevant to being spiritually reborn?

03
How do we "crucify the old man of sin?"

04
How does being born again allow us to see the kingdom of God, and why do we then desire to enter the kingdom?

05
Why must we be baptized and confirmed by one having authority in order to be born of the Spirit?

04

THE ABILITY TO SEE

As students, we often struggle with difficult concepts as we attempt to master worthwhile subjects in school. Frequently, in frustration, we may ask, "Why do I need to study this subject? I'll never use it again!" As we grow wiser, we begin to realize that even though these subjects may not seem relevant to us, over time we begin to see wisdom in studying them. One of the great advantages in receiving a higher education is learning how to see a greater good through the receipt of such knowledge acquired in college. This is also true with vocational education. As one enters the trades, they are apprenticed to someone who is a master of that trade. As they grow, they become known as "journeymen." Although they are not yet master craftsmen, they have accumulated enough knowledge to be successfully employed in the trade. As they acquire the ability to see comprehensively, they demonstrate this competence by passing examinations given by other master craftsmen. The underlying ability that is being tested is the ability to see problems as they really are and then provide a relevant solution.

In both cases, with the student who seeks higher education or the professional who seeks to become a master craftsman, the ability to see comes from recognition of the reality before us: we need to acquire knowledge from sources outside of ourselves. For the student, the principal purpose of his or her higher education is not to get a better job. While this is often the byproduct of their efforts, the primary goal of higher education is to make students better people, to give them the gift of sight. Likewise, for the professional, even though the goal is to become a master in the trade, that only occurs as the journeyman is able to see more clearly. To be able to see beyond oneself is a gift provided to us when we are humble and recognize our need for such information that must come from an outside source.

Consider the following example from scripture. We read of Elisha in 2 Kings 6. Here we read of war between Israel and Syria. In all of the preparations for war, experts were called on both sides. The king of Syria sought to capture Elisha, as he was prominent among those who were against him. He sent chariots and men to capture Elisha. We read in verse 14, *"Therefore sent he thither horses, and chariots, and a great host: and they came by night, and compassed the city about."* Here is where we learn that the need to see comes from outside ourselves. We read in verse 15, *"And when the servant of the man of God was risen early, and gone forth, behold, an host compassed the city both with horses and chariots. And his servant said unto him, Alas, my master! how shall we do?"*

It is now that the ability to see becomes critical. Elisha was the master craftsman; he was the gifted professor who had learned to be humble and to see beyond himself. He knew that true reality was found in sources outside of himself and he had learned how to access these sources. We read in verses 16–18, *"And he answered, Fear not: for they that be with us are more than they that be with them. And Elisha prayed, and said, LORD, I pray thee, open his eyes, that he may see. And the Lord opened the eyes of the young man; and he saw: and, behold, the mountain was full of horses and chariots of fire round about Elisha. And when they came down to him, Elisha prayed unto the LORD, and said, Smite this people, I pray thee, with blindness…"* The reason we need to acquire vision from our Heavenly Father is self-evident: matters pertaining to the soul are best handled by the Holy Ghost whose mission it is to enable us to see beyond ourselves.

We see that Elisha is a clear example of one who has been born again. He can see the kingdom of God and because of this, he is able to look to sources beyond himself for answers. We can rarely see these sources if we are fixed on matters of the self—matters that gratify our pride, matters that seek our self-interest. It is clear that in this world, we seek advantage through our ability to earn money or to develop our athletic abilities. These are good and useful. However, when it comes to the matters of our soul and the matters of heaven, we need a broader perspective. This perspective can only be obtained as we are born again and seek to see through the lens of Him in whose cause we seek to labor. Without His input, our labor is filled with self-advancement as we seek for a reward. This is not virtuous for it is not focused on a greater good.

VANITY CAUSES SPIRITUAL BLINDNESS

Our world is filled with telestial "tares," and so as we strive to be successful, we risk entering the realm of vanity. Benjamin Franklin is reported to have said, "Of all our infirmities, vanity is the dearest to us; a man will starve his other vices to keep that alive." The Lord hates vanity because when we are vain, we are selfish and unfit for His service. We read in Ecclesiastes 2:11, *"Then I considered all that my hands had done and the toil I had expended in doing it, and behold, all was vanity and a striving after wind, and there was nothing to be gained under the sun"* (English Standard Version). If we are vain, then our motives are vain; we cannot be born again in vanity. As we continue to observe human interaction, it becomes clear that vanity is a gateway sin and it invariably leads to the universal sin of pride.

From the words of our Lord we begin to "see" that we must put off these trappings of worldly success as measures of our spiritual success by being like a little child. Being able to access the Lord and find answers to our prayers is the first thing we must recognize as we heed the Lord's call to be born again. Such access is granted to those who are humble, even like a little child. How can we be born again of the Spirit if we can't recognize Him and our willingness so to do is conditioned upon real intent? This kind of intent comes when we are humble. Thus, we see that without real intent and without a willingness to be born again of the Spirit, we will not find answers to our prayers.

The Lord said we must be as a little child, metaphorically speaking, so that we can enter the kingdom of God. In the end, it will be only those who become like little children that will be able to be justified before God. Vanity is a condition of the soul that hardens the heart. This condition makes it impossible to feel the Spirit in our lives, and therefore precludes us from "seeing" the kingdom of God, let alone entering it. Consequently, it is as the Savior taught in the Sermon on the Mount, *"Blessed are the poor in spirit: for theirs is the kingdom of heaven.... Blessed are the meek: for they shall inherit the earth"* (Matthew 5:3 and 5). When we are meek and humble, we find hope in Christ; this empowers us to put off the natural man and we see the world beyond ourselves, as did Elisha.

We read in Mosiah 3:18, *"... but men drink damnation to their own souls except they humble themselves and become as little children, and believe that salvation was, and is, and is to come, in and through the atoning blood of Christ, the Lord Omnipotent."* Alma tells us what it means for us to be humble as he relates his born again experience. In Alma 36:5 we read, *"Now, behold, I say unto you, if I had not been born of God I should not have known these things; but God has, by the mouth of his holy angel, made these things known unto me, not of any worthiness of myself."* Alma is telling us that vanity and humility cannot abide together, and that humility is not defined as finding ourselves worthy, but rather relying on the Lord and His ability to make us worthy; this is where humility takes us.

By relying on the Lord and not on ourselves, we then focus our intent on Him and on His will; we then express this intent by our willingness to follow Him. We find ourselves harkening back to an earlier time, when we begin to remember the purity of relying solely on our Heavenly Father. That time was when we were children. We see children today and how they are filled with wonder as they learn an eternal truth purely; for the first time, they are overcome with wonderment. How excited we were to receive any nugget of truth when we were so young. So it now again must be. If we will but remember those occasions when we were very young, we will remember how excited we were to learn truth. The veil over our minds was not yet completely closed and in our innocence, we did not doubt. And, although we had yet to realize that it was the Holy Ghost in His pure form that gave us this truth, we just accepted it, for then we too were pure, not encumbered by the world.

Now, as we are older and held accountable for our actions, we realize we have fallen from that state of innocence. We have grown up, and with that, we have become skeptical of many things, and rightfully so. But in order to find real intent when it comes to finding answers to our prayers, we must return to that time when our hearts were pure. What a blessing it is to be baptized and receive the gift of the Holy Ghost! For we recognize that our baptism and confirmation allow us to be returned to a state of grace, meaning the effects of telestial living can be temporarily set aside. Then, as we partake of the sacrament worthily, we can once again be found justified before the Lord. It is in this condition that we can likewise find answers to our prayers, because we will now receive truth in that same state of wholesomeness we enjoyed so long ago.

How is this done? It is accomplished through the gift of the Holy Ghost who, when we worthily partake of those emblems, returns our lives to a state of cleanliness and innocence of the same magnitude found at our baptism. Remember the promise given to those who partake of the sacrament. At the end of each prayer we are promised, "*...that they may always have his Spirit to be with them*" (Doctrine and Covenants 20:77 and 79). It is the Holy Ghost who makes us able to be clean and humble, to indeed be like little children (see 2 Nephi 31:17). The Holy

Ghost is that greatest of gifts we received after our baptism, and by returning to the purity of a little child, we become able to activate the Spirit in such a way that we can find answers concerning our call to serve. Nephi confirms this in 2 Nephi 32:5, *"For behold, again I say unto you that if ye will enter in by the way, and receive the Holy Ghost, it will show unto you all things what ye should do."*

Vanity is the condition of the heart that leads us to be prideful, and since the "natural man" is the enemy of God (see Mosiah 3:19), is it unreasonable to conclude that vanity is the gateway sin that infests the soul with the very circumstances that allow pride to flourish? King Benjamin concludes in Mosiah 3:19, that the antidote for pride is having our souls return to that state where they are pure. He tells us that unless we yield to the promptings of the Holy Ghost, we cannot put off the natural man; we cannot be sanctified—meaning we cannot become a true saint—because the Atonement cannot heal us in our sins (see Alma 11:37). We must become like a little child, meek, humble and patient, and as we do so, when we partake of the sacrament, we can feel the effects of the events of being born again because the Lord's Spirit will be with us, as promised. It is then we will feel justified before God, not perfect, but justified because we can now see the kingdom of God through our faith. We will then know we have entered His kingdom through baptism and receiving the gift of the Holy Ghost.

It is then that we become willing to accept the love of God in whatever the Lord sees fit to inflict upon us. To do so requires faith and vision to see the kingdom of God by being born again. King Benjamin then tells us firmly, *"And behold, when that time cometh, none shall be found blameless before*

God, except it be little children, only through repentance and faith on the name of the Lord God Omnipotent" (Mosiah 3:21). There it is again, faith is linked with sight, just as the Lord taught Nicodemus. Unless a man is born again, he cannot see the kingdom of God.

FAITH EMPOWERS OUR WILLINGNESS TO SACRIFICE

The gift of the Holy Ghost will enable us to receive an answer to the questions we asked above concerning being a disciple—but is applicable to all Christ-centered service, and when we receive answers, we will feel them in our hearts and souls. We will be filled with peace and certainty concerning our service wherever it may be, and not just by an emotional response that induces behavior modification. Emotions must not be confused with the Spirit. While it is true we can have deep emotions when we feel the Spirit, truth taught by the Holy Ghost must bring with it a sense of peace and assurance. Isaiah taught us, *"And the work of righteousness shall be peace; and the effect of righteousness quietness and assurance for ever"* (Isaiah 32:17). We will recognize the influence of this great gift as He strengthens the soul and softens the heart and brings us peace and assurance through justification by the Spirit.

> **When we receive answers, we will feel them in our hearts and souls**

Our motive, which is everything, will now lead us to seek after real intent and by so doing we will also willingly seek for that answer. It is then that we will come to realize that willingness to receive the answer may require sacrifice. The need for sacrifice discloses the level of our faith. As we are prepared to sacrifice for our faith, we will be filled with the traits of patience, selflessness, and a desire that our decision be found acceptable to the Savior, for after all, it is into His service that we seek acceptance; it is in His service that we accept our errand from the Lord. Real intent and a willingness to learn from our Savior about what that errand might be are governed by following the promptings of the Holy Ghost. We may ask, "What kind of sacrifice does the Lord require to find answers?"

We confirm our willingness and our real intent to re-order our priorities as we seek the gift of faith. This is accomplished by showing the Lord we are willing to sacrifice whatever He requires of us. Let us read how this is done. In Alma 22:13 and 15 we read of Aaron's conversation with King Lamoni's father, *"And Aaron did expound unto him the scriptures from the creation of Adam, laying the fall of man before him, and their carnal state and also the plan of redemption... through Christ, for all whosoever would believe on his name.... And it came to pass that after Aaron had expounded these things unto him, the king said: What shall I do... that I may be born of God, having this wicked spirit rooted out of my breast, and receive his Spirit, that I may be filled with joy, that I may not be cast off at the last day? Behold, said he, I will give up all that I possess, yea, I will forsake my kingdom, that I may receive this great joy."* The king knew he had to make such a sacrifice for the Spirit.

Lamoni's father was willing to make that sacrifice to receive an answer to his prayer. He knew he needed to have his soul re-ordered to be "born of God." Notice the Lord did not actually require the king to give up his kingdom, but he did require the king to be willing to do so. King Lamoni's father was indeed willing to give up his kingdom and the Lord answered his prayer. In many cases, our willingness to sacrifice things of the world for those spiritual truths obtained by the Spirit will actually be required. This is not behavior modification, but true sacrifice of the world so that we might be born again; is this not what the Savior requires of us when He tells us we must be born again (see again John 3:3–5)?

This entire experience of Aaron and the king occurred because of the love King Lamoni had for Ammon (see Alma 20:26). And of course we know that the sons of Mosiah were converted because of the love their father had for them, then they were able to experience the love the Savior has for all men as the angel of the Lord visited them (see Mosiah 27:11–24). The sons of Mosiah were prepared to sacrifice their lives in the service of the Lamanites (see Alma 17:22–23). Then Alma the Younger testified on behalf of himself and the sons of Mosiah, as we read in Mosiah 27:25, *"And the Lord said unto me: Marvel not that all mankind, yea, men and women, all nations, kindreds, tongues and people, must be born again; yea, born of God, changed from their carnal and fallen state, to a state of righteousness, being redeemed of God, becoming his sons and daughters."*

So, if we are seeking the Lord's will concerning our service in His cause, we must not focus on the self; we must focus on Him and His ability to make us fit for His service, just as Lamoni and his father did. These are matters for the soul because the self often sees no benefit for the more impenetrable truths that pertain to our hearts. The self only sees value in a cost/benefit analysis where we weigh alleged benefits for the self against the costs required to receive these benefits. For example, are we willing to spend our lives in the service of God so that we can obtain wealth or power or a beautiful companion? Are we willing to submit to the rigors of being a disciple focusing on the Savior and not on ourselves?

Wealth and other worldly goods are not evil in and of themselves. However, these are not sufficient when trying to live a balanced life; if we seek them in preference to feeding the soul, when times get tough, as they will, these benefits are not sustainable. They do not feed us. Indeed, they blind us to the refining influence the Savior wants for our soul. And as this blindness increases, we will then "throw out" food for the soul as matters of the self becomes overpowering. We no longer seek to become like Him; we no longer seek to be made holy by the sacred fire of the Holy Ghost. Instead we abandon the soul to the self and its endless cost/benefit analyses.

BEING BORN OF THE SPIRIT CHANGES PRIORITIES

It is therefore very important that we look to our Savior and His life and see why He was meek and lowly in heart. His life will provide for us an example of how a life should be lived; moreover, when we study His life, we too will see that we will be able to find peace and answers in Him. His priorities become our priorities. We must acknowledge that it is in His service we wish to be made ready and thereby we will look to Him to provide peace—and equally important—answers to our prayers. We read in Matthew 11:29, *"Take my yoke upon you and learn from me; for I am gentle and lowly in heart, and you will find rest for your souls"* (Weymouth New Testament). We used the

Weymouth Version, as we have in other lessons for a reason. In our King James Version, we are told to "learn of me." In the Weymouth version, we are to learn "from" Him.

How are we to do that? The verse in both translations tells us how: because He is meek and lowly in heart and therefore, when we are likewise meek and lowly of heart, we will find rest to our soul. We will also find answers to our prayers. We know that sacrifice must be involved because inherent in our call to serve is a sacrifice of our time. Is there more? As we enhance our ability to follow the promptings of the Spirit, we will be led on a wonderful journey that will teach us things that we will use for the rest of our lives. We will come to know that the sacrifices the Lord requires are for our benefit as well as for the benefit of others. The sacrifices He requires makes us more fit for the kingdom so that we can be better used; these kinds of sacrifices are made so that we can both learn from Him and therefore be like Him.

We will find ourselves changing as we embrace the spiritual traits that abound in Him. We come to see that we might fulfill John's promise to us found in 1 John 3:2, *"Beloved, now are we the sons of God, and it doth not yet appear what we shall be: but we know that, when he shall appear, we shall be like him; for we shall see him as he is."* We cannot be like Him if we are not born again, for as we have learned from Him, all must be born again to see the kingdom of God, and all must be born again to inherit the kingdom of God. So, all must start at the very place young disciples contemplating service in His cause must begin. Everyone must start by seeking for real answers to meaningful prayers. The events of being born again are activated when we seek for answers, and to show our real intent and our willingness to truly receive an answer, we also learn to sacrifice the things of the world for the things of the Spirit. In that way, we become meek and lowly of heart; we show our willingness to receive His truth and the intent of our hearts is uncovered in sacrifice. As we pray for guidance, we learn from Him so that we eventually, over our lifetimes, can be like Him in that His attributes, things like faith, virtue, brotherly kindness, godliness and charity can be more plentifully found in us.

THE EXAMPLE OF OLIVER COWDERY

As we focus on the Lord and not on ourselves, we find new meaning in Oliver Cowdery's answer when he was seeking the Lord's mind and will. We begin to see how the Spirit answers questions concerning all kinds of service in the Lord's vineyard, including missionary service. In Doctrine and Covenants 6:14–15, the Lord explained to Oliver, *"Verily, verily, I say unto thee, blessed art thou for what thou hast done; for thou hast inquired of me, and behold, as often as thou hast inquired thou hast received instruction of my Spirit.... Behold, thou knowest that thou hast inquired of me and I did enlighten thy mind; and now I tell thee these things that thou mayest know that thou hast been enlightened by the Spirit of truth."* Here we see that once our intent is pure and real, we then begin, in faith, to understand and feel His Spirit. The events of being born again had commenced in Oliver Cowdery's life. As a result, the Lord told Oliver that when He speaks to him, such conversations enlighten his mind. Oliver will think new things and he will understand things that previously were confused in his mind. Things that seemed stuck would become unstuck.

As we begin to "see the kingdom of God," as did Nicodemus, so Oliver also began to feel his heart swell as his soul began to be re-ordered. With this experience, we at times also feel a "burning" within our hearts. We again read the Lord's counsel to Oliver Cowdery in Doctrine and Covenants 9:8, *"But, behold, I say unto you, that you must study it out in your mind; then you must ask me if it be right, and if it is right I will cause that your bosom shall burn within you; therefore, you shall feel that it is right."* This happens more often than not when we feel love and gratitude for God. Honestly, this does not happen all of the time, but if our hearts are right and we are humble, then what does happen all of the time is this: our minds are always enlightened! Is not this what Oliver Cowdery learned in Doctrine and Covenants 6?

Being enlightened by the Spirit happens as we grow in our ability to receive His word. With this ability, we are filled with confidence, peace, and determination to follow Him. This is the great "ah-hah"! These kinds of experiences start us on the path to being born again! As we recognize this enlightenment, we submit deeper requests to the Lord, and as we do so, we "study it out" with the help of the Spirit, and when we do so thoroughly, our hearts are moved with what the Lord described as a burning in the bosom. But for our purposes, as we seek answers in faith and as we are humble, we must realize that even without "studying it out," as we find real intent in being born again and as we approach the Lord in prayer, we then understand our minds are always enlightened by the Holy Ghost.

Sometimes we think that we can get someone to pray for us, someone who is more enlightened. Many Christians think we need to pray to someone else who can influence God. However, Paul taught that we need no intermediary when we pray if the events of being born again have commenced in our lives. If we are born again, we need no such intercessor. In Hebrews 4:16 we read, *"Let us therefore come boldly unto the throne of grace, that we may obtain mercy, and find grace to help in time of need."* Let us acknowledge our need to see and cultivate the ability so to do. As we have previously learned, we gain the ability to see as we are born again. We can see only as the Lord gives us sight by being born of the Spirit. This does not happen until we can come boldly to the throne of grace and see in Him, and Him alone, the key to our ability to navigate the perilous waters of life; it is in Him that our course is sure and it is in Him that we can let our light shine to those He wants us to serve.

BEING BORN AGAIN IS RARELY THEATRIC, BUT ALWAYS IMPRESSIVE

When the events of being born again commence, it is always because of our faith. Because of this, we need not seek for the spectacular. The Lord taught this lesson powerfully in the Old Testament. Let's consider the Lord's response to Elijah when he was seeking for answers. This experience also began with a prayer offered with real intent. As Elijah continued in prayer he too experienced this great "ah-hah." As Elijah taught us in 1 Kings 19:11–13, *"And he said, Go forth, and stand upon the mount before the LORD. And, behold the LORD passed by, and a great and strong wind rent the mountains, and brake in pieces the rocks before the LORD; but the LORD was not in the wind: and after the wind an earthquake; but the LORD was not in the earthquake: and after the earthquake a fire; but the LORD was not in the fire: and after the fire a still small voice. And it was so, when Elijah heard it, that he wrapped his face in his mantle, and went out...."* This still small voice does not always produce great physical manifestations of spiritual outpourings; nevertheless, it is the word of God to us and we must be able to have our hearts right to hear it. Our hearts are right if we are not filled with pride or vanity and if we seek to do God's will with a love for God's work. Mother Teresa once said, "There are few great events in life that will define greatness; only small events done with a great amount of love" (see *Mother Teresa—Come Be My Light*, pages 267–293).

> **Our hearts are right if we are not filled with pride or vanity and if we seek to do God's will**

When we adopt this attitude, our hearts are right before our Heavenly Father. The Spirit comes with His "still small voice" and it is this that we seek. The Holy Ghost can produce an emotional response, but more often and more predictably, it comes with the feelings of peace and strength, not crying or emoting. If it seems that we are overly emotional, we might be putting our desires to please others before we have adequately allowed the Spirit to fill our hearts with His truth. Isaiah taught us, *"But they that wait upon the LORD shall... mount up with wings as eagles; they shall run, and not be weary; and they shall walk, and not faint"* (Isaiah 40:31). When we begin to seek after the still small voice, we begin to see things differently; we begin to have elevated thoughts as we contemplate His great work. We find ourselves steeped in patience and understanding, with a desire to seek additional knowledge. We don't expect great manifestations, but instead we look for and expect the regular communication promised to all as exemplified by the answer the Lord gave to Oliver Cowdery.

As we begin to be born of the Spirit and "see the kingdom of God," we then know that the Spirit of the Lord is with us; we feel His pleasure in our actions for our minds are enlightened, and we are justified before Him (see Mosiah 4:8–12). Our love for the Savior is increasing; great and momentous decisions can now be reached. We read in Alma 37:6–7, *"Now ye may suppose that this is foolishness in me; but behold I say unto you, that by small and simple things are great things brought to pass; and small means in many instances doth confound the wise. And the Lord God doth work by means to bring about his great and eternal purposes; and by very small means the Lord doth confound the wise and bringeth about the salvation of many souls."* President Spencer W. Kimball explained in 1973:

> The burning bushes, the smoking mountains... the Cumorahs and the Kirtlands were realities but they were the exceptions. The great volume of revelation comes... in the less spectacular way—that of deep impressions without spectacle or dramatic events. Always expecting the spectacular, many will surely miss entirely the constant flow of communication (Conference Report, Munich Area Conference, 1973 as reported in *Doctrine and Covenants and Church History Seminary Teachers Resource Manuel,* page 77).

President Joseph Fielding Smith continues:

> A manifestation of an angel would not leave the impression as firmly as if we receive truth by the power of the Holy Ghost. Personal visitations might become dim as times goes on, but this guidance of the Holy Ghost is renewed and

continued day after day, year by year, if we live worthy of it (*Doctrines of Salvation,* 1:44).

Every time we ask the Lord with real intent, He enlightens our minds. This happens not sometimes, but every time. We just need to be made ready to receive this communication by returning to a state of innocence, which comes when we worthily partake of the sacrament and seek His face in humility. There are certainly times when the Lord does speak miraculously. When these kinds of communications happen, we must remember the Lord's counsel, *"Remember that that which cometh from above is sacred, and must be spoken with care, and by constraint of the Spirit"* (Doctrine and Covenants 63:64). To this point, Elder Boyd K. Packer stated:

> Dreams, visions and visitations are not uncommon in the Church in this dispensation. It may be that you will be the recipient of a marvelous spiritual experience. I have come to know that these experiences are personal.... Ponder them in your heart and do not talk lightly about them ("The Great Plan of Happiness and Personal Revelation," [CES Fireside for Young Adults, November 9, 1993, *Missionary Preparation Manual* 2005, pages 21–30).

QUESTIONS ABOUT THE LESSON

01
How does the Holy Ghost allow us to see beyond ourselves?

02
What needs to happen in order to "see the kingdom of God?"

03
What is vanity and why does the Lord hate it?

04
How do we learn from the Savior as opposed to learning of Him?

05
Why is learning by the Spirit the sure way to enlightenment and preferable to visions and dreams?

05

THE NEED FOR A BROKEN HEART AND A CONTRITE SPIRIT

Once, many years ago, there was a young man from Mexico who was seeking ways he could respond to the call to serve. He had received an answer to his prayers regarding missionary service, but was considering either a service mission or a full-time proselyting mission. However, the young man was poor and because he was poor, he thought he would not be able to serve. He wrote to Church headquarters with his dilemma. His plea concerning his pending mission came to the attention of President Spencer W. Kimball. One day, as President Kimball was having his hair cut at the Deseret Barber Shop where he made brother Ross Pyper aware of this young man's concerns. President Kimball knew that Ross was a collector of rare coins, and as President Kimball had ascertained from this young man's priesthood leaders, the young potential missionary had accumulated quite a collection of valuable coins. These coins had been shipped by the young potential missionary to President Kimball and now he asked if Ross would come to his office later that afternoon and give the prophet an assessment as to their value.

Brother Pyper did as President Kimball requested, and appeared at his office later that day. The coins were on President Kimball's sideboard. President Kimball told Ross that he had a meeting elsewhere and Ross was free to spend whatever time he needed to evaluate the coins. When President Kimball returned, Ross was to give him a monetary number as to their value. By the time he returned, Ross had finished his evaluation. He told President Kimball what he determined the value of these coins to be. President Kimball thanked Ross and looked at the sum Brother Pyper had written down and nodded his head in the affirmative. He then told Ross that he thought the price was fair, and then quite surprisingly, asked Ross to buy the entire collection at that very price Ross himself had determined.

Ross was surprised, but because President Kimball had asked him so to do, he wrote President Kimball a check and took possession of the coins. Brother Pyper was puzzled by all of this and asked President Kimball why, when this potential missionary was otherwise so poor, did we need to relieve him of this asset; surely others could help pay for the young man's mission. President Kimball thoughtfully responded to Ross. He explained that in order for the young man's mission to be truly meaningful, sacrifice was required. He hoped all missionaries would realize that sacrifice, even if it hurts, would focus our intent to serve the Lord for the right reasons. It was only as the young missionary sacrificed his worldly possessions that his heart became contrite and his spirit more sensitive to the will of the Lord.

The months since Brother Pyper bought the coins turned into years. And at the end of the second year, Ross realized the young missionary was about to return. He had kept those certain coins separate from other coins in his collection. When President Kimball came to the barbershop for a haircut, Ross enquired of him. He told President Kimball that the coins had greatly appreciated in value and asked if it wouldn't be appropriate for him to pay the young missionary that increase, as the missionary was certain to need funds at the end of his mission. President Kimball responded by telling Ross he had done as the prophet had requested and the matter was closed.

SACRIFICING THE SELF FOR THE SOUL

This illustration teaches us an important point about sacrifice. Had Brother Pyper returned the increase to the missionary, the required sacrifice would not have had its purifying influence in the young missionary's life. In order to obtain a broken heart and a contrite spirit, we must be willing to put matters of the soul before matters of the self. The young man from Mexico had sold the coins to finance his own mission, a clear sacrifice of worldly goods for spiritual gain. To now return to him the increase in value of the coins would only communicate to him that the sacrifice he had made was only a simulated one and in the end, a total commitment to sacrifice was not necessary. It wasn't really needed. Should that occur, it would give the missionary the wrong idea. The young missionary decided to sacrifice these worldly treasures for spiritual ones. He did so because he sought to obtain a broken heart, a heart that would be able to receive a greater portion of the Spirit.

The sacrifice of worldly treasure for the growth provided by the mission is priceless! President Kimball was not going to compromise this fact by telling this young missionary that even this great sacrifice of physical wealth to go on his mission was somehow a trick. It was somehow an illusion and that if he would just go along with it, in reality, the worldly goods would be increased. This is not a good connection to make. While it is true the Lord does bless us with material goods, even increases, He does so only if these increases do not compromise our spiritual growth. If such increases occur without the Lord's consent, and sometimes this happens, then pride and the enlargement of the self is the result. If the appreciation of the coins was paid to the missionary, it might signify that the value of the coins was more important than the spiritual gifts he had received.

We often do not know what the Lord may require of us, but we do know that sacrifice is always part of our walk with Christ. We see sacrifice when we fast, we see sacrifice when we pay our tithing, and we see sacrifice when we give our time to His work. In the above example, President Kimball recognized that for this young missionary, he needed to sacrifice his coin collection so that he might serve a mission. It is clear that this young man grew immeasurably because he realized the value of this missionary experience exceeded the market value of the coins. This is a lesson we all could learn. The young man was able to see that time spent in the service of our Savior was so much more valuable than time spent in worldly pursuits.

Why would this be so? By sacrificing this prized possession, the young man gained perspective; such a sacrifice of material goods as well as the sacrifice of time in the unique call to full-time missionary service allowed the young man to retreat from the world. Even if it were only for twenty-four months, it would give him time to grow. For most of us, full-time service in the work of the Lord comes infrequently, but the call to be a young disciple matures the young man or young woman well beyond any time spent as a missionary. The growth that such service gives to us cannot be truly measured. When we come to understand this growth, we would pay any worldly price to receive this tutoring from the Savior.

In such an environment, like that of full-time missionary service but truly in any setting where a disciple of Christ is needed, it is possible to learn closely the ways of God. During this time of service, the young man or woman could develop his or her ability to call on God and to hear His voice clearly in response. They could then understand how the Lord deals with His children and how His Spirit works in a world where knowledge of God and His gospel has been lost. It is a time where the young man or young woman could grow and become someone greater than his or her abilities, even if it were only for a season. He or she would learn how to navigate mortality successfully. They would learn that their lives, like all lives, are fragile and should be handled with prayer.

They would learn how much the Lord cares for all His children, and they would also learn how much God cares for His young disciples in all conditions of service. They would also know that to be asked to sacrifice in the Lord's service provides to any young disciple a gift like no other—the gift to glimpse the mind of God and to have their understanding elevated. Such disciples of Christ would truly see the will of God at work.

The benefits that President Kimball sought to impress on the young Mexican brother are applicable to all young disciples.

They are often lost in a world that seems ever more secular and where life is constantly measured in terms of immediate cost/benefit analysis. They would realize that the greatest benefits of a mission are spiritual in the sense that if completed with the Lord's approval and commenced with the events of being born again, then such a missionary's faith would begin to be unshakeable and he or she would come to truly know matters that pertain to the soul; is this not a singularly good reason to seek to be born again?

President Kimball has shown us in this example of the young man from Mexico and his desire to have a productive mission, how to cultivate the ability to "see the kingdom of God"—to begin the events that cause us to be born again (see John 3:3–5)—and to access the libraries of heaven. Such access requires sacrifice, even the sacrifice of worldly possessions to obtain such knowledge. Let's look at the father of King Lamoni in the Book of Mormon. He was willing to give up his kingdom so that he might acquire the ability to see the kingdom of God. In both cases, President Kimball's and the case of King Lamoni's father, it becomes extremely pertinent that we be willing to sacrifice things of the world for the incomparable treasures that belong to the kingdom of heaven.

If we are not willing to sacrifice worldly treasures for heavenly ones, we run a substantial risk

Why is this so? It is because if we are not willing to sacrifice worldly treasures for heavenly ones, we run a substantial risk of combining that which is not able to be combined: we seek to value material blessings as part of our spiritual endowment. In other words, we do not differentiate between material blessings and the spiritual endowment given to us by being born again; we think that we might re-order our soul and face the light by embracing material blessings as part of our spiritual legacy. This is Calvinism, pure and simple. We see in Calvinism, or Reformed Christianity, an interesting doctrine. Calvinists believe in a limited Atonement: Christ's sacrifice will be valid only for the elect. Moreover, even though Calvinists believe in being saved by grace—as do we—they see this grace only applied to the elect. Hence, we get hints that we are the elect in the form of material blessings given to us, as God is in charge of all wealth. Accordingly, it follows that He gives us riches and other worldly blessings as a reward for our faithfulness. This is Calvinism at its best because it creates a connection between wealth and God's favor. While we know that our Heavenly Father is the author of all blessings, even wealth, it is when we think wealth is an indicator of God's favor that we run into trouble.

THE ANTIDOTE TO PRIDE

What does it mean to have a broken heart and a contrite spirit? Elder Bruce D. Porter, in his conference address in October 2007, gave us a very good definition: "Those who have a broken heart and a contrite spirit are willing to do anything and everything God asks of them" ("A Broken Heart and a Contrite Spirit," *Ensign,* November 2007, page 31). When we are willing to do what the Lord wants of us, not what we always desire, we become meek and teachable. The operative word is "willing." We have already studied in the previous lessons what it means to have real intent, and in that context we know that real intent and being willing are irretrievably linked. To be a true disciple of Christ we become very aware that the Lord requires a commitment of us to Him. To this point, the Lord told the brethren in Kirtland, *"Behold, the Lord requireth the heart and a willing mind..."* (Doctrine and Covenants 64:34).

Why did He say this? It is because our Savior was willing to do the will of the Father perfectly. This was His real intent. His heart was broken because His will was "broken" and completely subordinate to the will of the Father. We read in John 12:49, *"Because I have not spoken on my own authority; but the Father who sent me, Himself gave me a command what to say and in what words to speak"* (Weymouth New Testament). So, we can now say, also irretrievably, a broken heart is not exemplified if we desire to "impress" the Lord with our obedience in the sense that we seek to earn blessings.

No, our obedience now becomes sacred to us and held closely between the Lord and ourselves; it is not for public consumption. We realize that when we are obedient, we feel the Lord's Spirit with us, and this creates a space between the world and us. It is in this space, created by our faith and followed up by our obedience, that we find God. Because we have brought forth such a sacrifice of a broken heart and a contrite spirit, our willingness to be obedient is to glorify God, not ourselves. In that way, obedience becomes a matter of the soul and not of the self. Accordingly, we have learned to rely on the Lord and to go quietly about His business, even though we do so as an unprofitable servant (see Mosiah 2:21 and Luke 17:5–10).

Rudyard Kipling wrote of a broken heart and a contrite spirit in 1897 when he penned these lines in his poem, *Recessional:*

> The tumult and the shouting dies;
> The captain and the kings depart;
> Still stands thine ancient sacrifice,
> An humble and a contrite heart.

The Savior Himself possessed the ultimate broken heart, and as a result, performed the ultimate sacrifice that He and He alone could make as He died on Calvary. His will was completely swallowed up in the will of the Father and in that manner of complete surrender to the Father's will, He quietly brought forth the sacrifice of sacrifices that redeemed all men and women. This is the example He wishes us to follow. Not one that is spectacular, to be seen of men. Do we not suppose that if spectacular was needed, He could have been so spectacular that it would have destroyed the need for faith? To that end, we must remember that His sacrifice was made in a small place called Judea, and His life was lived in the backwaters of the Roman Empire. He did not destroy our faith because faith is the power that God uses to do His work. Even though the world took little note of Him in His time, it was changed by Him through His faith.

Why is this so? It is because the Son of God made the ultimate sacrifice for us. His sacrifice was accomplished because He truly died of a broken heart (see *Jesus The Christ,* page 669, note 8). The antidotes to pride are the broken heart and the contrite spirit. This sacrifice keeps us from being tainted by the world; the scales of blindness that prejudice the natural man to favor the things of the world are removed. It is then that we become willing to do whatever the Lord requires of us. It is then that we are able to keep ourselves unspotted from the world. When we have a broken heart and a contrite spirit we are able to receive grace from our Savior and repent of our sins.

We also look forward to His promise of redemptive faith as He promised those who have a broken heart in 1 Corinthians 12:9. With the broken heart, our souls begin to be re-ordered and we view our Savior as both the subject and object of our faith. Moreover, those who possess a broken heart and a contrite spirit desire to acquire His qualities of faith, hope, virtue, patience, godliness, and most importantly, charity. These are the attributes of meekness and when we possess them, they make us "fruitful in the knowledge of Jesus Christ" (see 2 Peter 1:4–7). This is why Abinadi explained to us that if we are born again, we are His seed; and as we become possessed of the attributes of faith, hope and charity, we can then embrace a fullness of His being. We read in Mosiah 15:10, *"... Behold, I say unto you, that when his soul has been made an offering for sin he shall see his seed. And now what say ye? Who are his seed?"*

Abinadi then goes on to explain why the broken heart and the contrite spirit are absolute prerequisites to being born again, and by inference, tells us we then become the seed of Christ. In verses 11–12 we read, *"Behold I say unto you, that whosoever has heard the words of the prophets, yea, all the holy prophets who have prophesied concerning the coming of the Lord—I say unto you, that all those who have hearkened unto their words, and believed that the Lord would redeem his people, and have looked forward to that day for a remission of their sins, I say unto you, that these are his seed, or they are heirs of the kingdom of God. For these are they whose sins he has borne; these are they for whom he has died, to redeem them from their transgressions. And now, are they not his seed?"* This is how the scriptures refer to those who have been born again: they are redeemed as the seed of Christ. This rebirth comes through their faith, received as a gift when they have brought forth the sacrifice of a broken heart and a contrite spirit. Then, the Lord can bear their burdens and relieve them of the effects of their sins.

Josephus, the great Jewish and Roman historian, is the only intellectual of that time that even noted our Savior's existence, and then only barely. This was because the Savior was interested in humility, not in making Himself great. He is great because He is the Son of God; on its face that is a great state of being. The sacrifices of a broken heart and a contrite spirit are of eternal duration. They are sacrifices required by the Savior to be made quietly and privately in the deep recesses of our hearts and souls. They are not sacrifices that call attention to ourselves, but are worked out secretly in the hidden chambers found in a great Gethsemane known only to us. The sacrifice of the broken heart and the contrite spirit is found only in our own hearts where such sacrifice has enduring and everlasting purpose.

A broken heart and a contrite spirit are to be made quietly and privately in the deep recesses of our hearts and souls

ESAU AND JACOB: CONTRASTING REWARDS

To illustrate why equating blessings of the self—blessings of wealth and worldly position—to those of the soul do not embrace the needs of the soul nor do they embrace our Lord's understanding of things as they really are, let us look at the story of Jacob and Esau. We see in this example of how the spiritual blindness of Esau was of greater consequence than the literal blindness of Isaac when he blessed his sons. Jacob and Esau were twins and both sons of Isaac who was the son of Abraham. The Abrahamic covenant had been given to Isaac (see Genesis 26:2–3) and in the beginning, Isaac preferred Esau to Jacob. This was due to the fact that Esau was a hunter and a man possessed of worldly talents.

In Genesis 25:30–34, we read, *"And Esau said to Jacob, Feed me, I pray thee, with that same red pottage; for I am faint.... And Jacob said, Sell me this day thy birthright. And Esau said, Behold, I am at the point to die: and what profit shall this birthright do to me? And Jacob said, Swear to me this day; and he sware unto him: and he sold his birthright unto Jacob. Then Jacob gave Esau bread and pottage of lentiles; and he did eat and drink, and rose up, and went his way: thus Esau despised his birthright."* Esau conflated his birthright with worldly rewards and valued it below that of earthly rewards, and thus, he valued it as less than nothing. Contrast this example with that of King Lamoni's father, who was willing to give up his entire kingdom, so dear was it to him to be born again. Jacob, on the other hand, was able to separate worldly rewards from those obtained by the Spirit; Jacob sought to be born again, to both see the kingdom of God and enter that kingdom. Esau sought after the pleasures of this world.

Why did Esau do this, and are there not many who are like him? The answer is yes, there are many like Esau, and here is why. We read a familiar refrain about telestial living in Mosiah 3:19, *"For the natural man is an enemy to God, and has been from the fall of Adam, and will be, forever and ever, unless he yields to the enticings of the Holy Spirit, and putteth off the natural man and becometh a saint through the atonement of Christ the Lord..."* Mortality inevitably brings with it the traits of the natural man. Mortality provides an existence where it is so very easy for us to confuse the riches of this world with the riches of the Spirit. Calvinism has been doing it for 500 years! But this conflation has deadly consequences, as we saw with Esau. The land that Esau's descendants came to inhabit was known in Old Testament times as the Land of Edom, not a land flowing with milk and honey; they did not inherit Isaac's birthright and so they had to look to Jacob, or Israel for salvation.

We are free to choose, to follow this inclination to be the natural man or, if we desire to plumb the libraries of heaven and drink from the waters of life provided by the Savior, we must choose to sacrifice the things of the world in favor of the things of the Spirit. This is not an either/or proposition, but we must be always willing to give up the things of this world so that we might gain the ability to re-order our soul and feed our hearts. This only happens when our spirits are contrite and our hearts broken. Sacrifice requires us to make a conscious choice to do so. Why would we choose to sacrifice the world for the things of heaven when the world and its pleasures seem so immediately convenient, abundant, and within our grasp? The Lord knows this and so he gave us the law of sacrifice. In Old Testament times, this law was fulfilled with the sacrifice of animals on the altar. Today however, the Lord has taught us in Doctrine and Covenants 59:8, *"Thou shalt offer a sacrifice unto the Lord thy God in righteousness, even that of a broken heart and a contrite spirit."*

Things of the Spirit seem distant and are not readily seen by us in our current mortal state. There really is no immediate benefit that can be measured; spiritual blessings of faith, virtue, and charity offer us hope in the "by and by," but rarely do they have any immediate "cash value," although we try hard to create such. We think that the world will pay more for a virtuous person, and it probably will. We teach that if we are virtuous, we will earn more money. It is in this kind of a comparison that the conflation between the things of the Spirit and the things of the world is best seen. We can measure immediate results with the things of the world. If this is our focus, behold, as the Savior said of seeking worldly acknowledgement with respect to virtue or any other spiritual trait, "You have your reward."

AVOID CONFUSING WORLDLY GAINS WITH SPIRITUAL GAINS

The Lord taught in Matthew 6:1, *"Be careful not to practice your righteousness in front of others to be seen by them. If you do, you will have no reward from your Father in heaven"* (New International Version). And to put the whole matter of this confusion to rest, He said, *"No man can serve two masters: for either he will hate the one, and love the other; or else he will hold to the one, and despise the other. Ye cannot serve God and mammon"* (Matthew 6:24). If we try to serve two masters, what we discover is this: we see immediate benefits if we modify our behavior; we get thinner, we gain more energy, or we find immediate financial rewards in steps to success as our income rises. In this way we have linked the things of the world with the things of God. We see that in the world, the law of sacrifice points to deferred gratification only so that our reward will be enhanced when it arrives; with spiritual matters, it seems that they are to be acquired for success in the next life.

They are so transcendental and otherworldly. To possess these kinds of spiritual attributes might even make us less likely to enjoy the success of the world and its abundant bounty. Those who feel this way often ask, "In order to enjoy success in this world is it really necessary to know the mind of God?" The premise of this question is this: can this knowledge, the ability to "see the kingdom of God," be translated immediately into worldly blessings? If not, then we often say, "I'll wait until after I am a success in the world, and then I'll seek for spiritual knowledge."

This is a grave error and an act of folly that has eternal consequences. If we believe in this direct connection between obedience and wealth, we don't see any immediate benefit above perfunctory obedience to the commandments so that we might check the box. By so doing, are we not like Esau? While there are many verses in scripture that tell us if we keep the commandments we shall prosper in the land (see Mosiah 2:22, Alma 36:30, Leviticus 26, and Deuteronomy 28), to prosper in this sense may have a multitude of meanings. It is generally true that the obedient do prosper in the land, meaning that the Lord will provide for their worldly welfare; it does not mean He will make them rich.

However, if we torture these meanings to seek a direct correlation to being made rich, we err. Do we not think when we check the box that we are earning our blessings? Those who think this way misunderstand the following verse found in Jacob 2:19, *"And after ye obtained a hope in Christ ye shall obtain riches, if ye seek them; and ye will seek them for the intent to do good—to clothe the naked, and to feed the hungry, and to liberate the captive, and administer relief to the sick and the afflicted."* If we invert the order and seek riches first, it is a sure bet we will not administer relief to the sick nor will we feed the hungry. Our attention will be focused on the self and surely not on the soul, and as such, our soul will remain unfed and in a desperate, if unseen, need of spiritual relief.

NO DIRECT LINK BETWEEN RICHES AND OBEDIENCE

In our world of capitalism today, we often think that life is a marketplace in which we create wealth by "doing good." The problem arises because we see a direct link between riches and seeking for them. We think that if we intend to administer relief to the sick, for example, by merely measuring our attendance on church records, or proffering our tithing receipts, we have checked the box and have hope in Christ. Those who think this way are now free to seek riches with reckless abandon as they seek to bind God in an unholy alliance to become wealthy. Those who are inclined to make any sacrifice so that they may obtain the things of the world see in this verse a prescription that almost ensures wealth. They erroneously think that by being obedient, they will be wealthy. Of course they say, "We will feed the sick and clothe the naked, just make us wealthy first!"

People who believe this way are not born again and do not see the kingdom of God at all. This is excessive pride at the very least and complete self-absorption, clothed in arrogance, at worst. What those who make a direct link from intent to wealth fail to realize is this: the real relationship between riches and seeking after them is an indirect one. If we do not keep the acquisition of wealth separate from seeking after our Savior, then He will never become the subject of our faith. We must be willing to sacrifice the things of the world and its riches for that state of being known to the soul as being born again. The need to be willing to sacrifice the things of the world is lost on those of us who think there is a direct link between wealth and righteousness. They fall into a spiritual trap; they fall into the ranks of the blind. It is the height of the "do good and earn blessings" deviation to link obedience directly to earning blessings, especially wealth.

As we begin to experience the events of being born again, we "see the kingdom of God." And when we do, we realize that there is no way, by our own actions, we can qualify to enter His kingdom. Of course we must accept His gift of salvation, and that requires us to do those things that make us more like our Savior so that we can enter His kingdom. We must also cease to make a direct link between obedience to specific commandments and the earning of specific blessings, like wealth. We realize such a direct link does not exist. We realize that as the events of being born again commence, great sacrifice and even suffering may be required.

Once we "see the kingdom of God," we understand that we must enter this kingdom through the gate of baptism, or, if we have already been baptized, we desire to unlock our access to the gift of the Holy Ghost and we start to see our priorities being re-ordered to reflect His desires and needs. Our vision has thus been elevated. When this happens, we no longer hunger for wealth; we no longer seek to feed our earthly appetites because we desire something better. If we make a direct link to riches, we will find our ability to see the kingdom of God becomes blurred and our spiritual rebirth is stopped. If this be the case, how do such think they shall enter, and unless they are able to "see the kingdom," how do we suppose they shall find the gate?

They misunderstand Jacob because they think in terms of earthly rewards first; they see keeping the commandments as a prelude for riches and worldly success. Because Jacob foresaw this difficulty, he added the next verse (Jacob 2:20), *"And now, my brethren, I have spoken unto you concerning pride; and those of you which have afflicted your neighbor, and persecuted him because ye were proud in your hearts, of the things which God hath given you, what say ye of it?"* We find Jacob of the Book of Mormon diagnosing a common malady of the soul, which is like Jacob of the Old Testament. Jacob, the son of Lehi tells us that far from finding a direct link to wealth, we must be reconciled to Christ. If we seek for wealth only—or for power, prestige, or followers—we are like Esau: we suffer from spiritual hoof and mouth disease.

THE DANGER OF PRIDE

Those diagnosed with pride seek to conform to the commandments, but they are not truly obedient. In order to escape the conformity trap and render sighted obedience, we must be born of the Spirit and acquire faith in the Lord Jesus Christ. Without faith in our Savior, we cannot see the kingdom of God. In this condition, we suffer from Esau's malady and are not born again, nor are we willing to make any sacrifice whatsoever, unless it has an earthly benefit. The root of Esau's malady is pride. The Lord finds pride particularly distasteful as he tells us in Proverbs 16:18, *"Pride goeth before destruction, and an haughty spirit before a fall."* Is this not the very condition in which Esau found himself? King Benjamin warned us that the natural man is the enemy of God precisely because of the sin of pride.

Jacob is very clear above: pride is an affliction of the heart, and the Lord told us it is the nature and disposition of almost all men to exercise unrighteous dominion over others because of pride (see Doctrine and Covenants 121:39). Alexander Solzhenitsyn wrote, in his trilogy about the repressive Soviet prison system, "Pride grows in the human heart like lard on a pig" (*The Gulag Archipelago—1918–1956,* I and II). As we can see, pride is indeed the universal sin. We read that pride in our hearts always deceives us (see Obadiah 1:3); thus, pride always blinds us to the truth. It promises honor and riches, but it delivers uncertainty and fleeting success.

During Roman times, when a great conquest was made, the Prefect or Imperator rode in a chariot to accept the emperor's congratulations for his victory. The streets of the Appian Way were lined with admiring Romans cheering this great leader and honoring him for his victory. The road led to the emperor where he would be crowned with a laurel of victory, placed on his head by the emperor himself. As he listened to the accolades of victory, there was always a slave riding with the conqueror and whispering in his ear, "All glory is fleeting," lest the victor feel himself invincible. So it is with all earthly rewards: they are all fleeting. This is why the Book of Proverbs declares that pride precedes destruction (Proverbs 16:18).

> **It promises honor and riches, but it delivers uncertainty and fleeting success**

We have learned previously that we run the risk of vanity if we are not willing to sacrifice worldly gain for spiritual truth. But now, as we embrace irresolutely the praise of the world and the success it brings, we see that vanity can become a form of spiritual cancer. This hyper form of vanity is seen everywhere; it is eating away at our ability to see the kingdom of God, and also blinds us to our own interests. We read in Proverbs 26:12, *"Do you see a man who is wise in his own eyes? There is more hope for a fool than for him"* (English Standard Version).

What is the remedy for such a condition, or does it last forever? There is an antidote and it is found in what King Benjamin told us: we must "put off the natural man" through the Atonement of Christ. Unless we accept His Atonement offered through His generous grace, the condition does last forever. We have already learned we must be willing to sacrifice the things of this world for the blessings of heaven so that we might "see the kingdom of God" by being born again, but there is more. We must have the ability to make a sacrifice of the self for the redemption of the soul. Moreover, as the events of spiritual rebirth begin, we soon see that sacrifices, those made to receive answers to our prayers, give us vision to continue these sacrifices for deeper significance. We sacrifice the self for the soul and in so doing we focus on the gift of faith.

QUESTIONS ABOUT THE LESSON

01
What is sacrifice and why is it necessary for worship?

02
What specifically do I need to sacrifice so that my heart will be broken and my spirit contrite?

03
What is the definition of a broken heart and a contrite spirit and why are these the building blocks of faith?

04
How do we sacrifice the things of the world correctly?

05
Why is the link between riches and obedience an indirect one?

06

FAITH IS A GIFT

There are many examples of heroic rescues and feats of improbable strength that illustrate the lengths we go to save lives. One such incident occurred between October 14–16, 1987, when an 18-month old little girl fell into a well in her aunt's backyard. Rescuers worked nonstop for 58 hours to free her from the eight-inch well casing, 22 feet below the ground. The story gained worldwide attention as the efforts of these rescuers were reported multiple times during the day. All efforts were made and the world watched with baited breath as the rescuers attempted to free little Jessica McClure from the well that could have become the little girl's grave. All new technology was employed, even water-jet cutting to free her. The entire world was transfixed upon the events in Midland, Texas, for more than two days in October 1987. The news of Jessica's rescue was the lead news story when the rescuers freed her from that pit. It was one day when good news filled the world with joy.

We were all thrilled at baby Jessica's rescue. She had been given the gift of life by these rescuers who were not about to give up. This precious gift of life was given by those who appreciated her circumstances and who did not seek for any special monetary reward; in other words, baby Jessica did not need to do anything to receive this precious gift. They gave her an unconditional, intangible gift that she herself could not earn, nor could she do anything that would warrant the rescuer's attention. They performed their life-giving act because they felt one life was precious. This is the role of the Savior; He stepped down to rescue us (see 1 Nephi 11:16–22).

What does this story tell us about gifts? It tells us that gifts are given to us because of the largess of the giver, not because the receiver earned the gift or merited it in any way. Gifts are different than awards. When one is given an award, it is because of some meritorious service or act. This is best shown in the academic world when honorary doctorates are bestowed on outstanding individuals who have blessed the lives of many others as a result of their sacrifices on behalf of others or because of the sacrifices they themselves have made to advance the knowledge in their chosen field of interest. Such service is thereby recognized.

Gifts are different from prizes. They are given because the giver of the gift wants to bestow knowledge, wealth, or something very precious on the receiver. These kinds of gifts are often called endowments. Gifts endow the recipient with something they themselves cannot earn while awards enrich those who receive them precisely because of the things they have achieved. We often confuse these terms in a spiritual sense. We think that when the Lord uses the word "gift," He really means, "award."

This is not true. When the Lord uses the word "gift," He means it. The point is best understood when we look at the words of Paul found in Romans 6:23, *"For the wages of sin is death; but the gift of God is eternal life through Jesus Christ our Lord."* Here we see that wages, or "earnings," are equated with sin. We earn our damnation through committing sin and then not repenting of these sins. We receive eternal life from our Savior as a gift when we repent and feed our souls. We accept His gift by being born again of the water and the Spirit. It means the rejection of the awards of the world in favor of the gifts of the Spirit. Would we ever expect to be awarded an honorary doctorate of laws or letters because we received the gift of eternal life given as an endowment to us by the Savior's efforts? Certainly we do not redeem ourselves! Accordingly, we must ask, upon what criteria is the gift given? Many think we must earn eternal life, but Paul was very clear that earning is associated with sin and not with eternal life; the gift of eternal life is given because of the generosity of the Giver!

We can say then, that we are awarded our final destination if we have not been born again, because we have earned or merited such an award. Being born again, as we have learned in Lesson Three, requires us to turn away from the world of reward and prizes and live according to the Spirit. When we are born again and can see the kingdom of God, we will desire to enter it. We acknowledge that should we receive eternal life, it will be as Lehi taught us in 2 Nephi 2:8, *"... that they may know that there is no flesh that can dwell in the presence of God, save it be through the merits, and mercy, and grace of the Holy Messiah..."* Eternal life is a gift in every sense, not an award. Receiving the gift of eternal life acknowledges that such is beyond our ability to "earn" it. Eternal life must be given, as a gift, from Him who bought us with His blood, for it is He and not we who paid the price for eternal life.

Many who confuse the terms "gift" and "award" turn to 2 Nephi 25:23, which reads, *"For we labor diligently to write, to persuade our children, and also our brethren, to believe in Christ, and to be reconciled to God; for we know that it is by grace that we are saved, after all we can do."* They seem to think that grace is given after we do our part and by implication, our part means we must be completely obedient to all statutes, laws, and commandments before we can merit His grace or His gift of eternal life. There is that word again, "merit." This highlights the confusion. In this light, can we not see that we have created an exchange value, a transactional value like ones we find in business? We exchange our obedience for His work and by so doing are we not creating an equality of our works with His work? There have been those who have analogized this verse to mean we must do ninety percent of the work of salvation and then, because we are not able to do it all, the Lord will make up the difference. Thus, we have done "all" we can do. This is Calvinism pure and simple; such an understanding is inconsistent with the restored gospel and not consistent with the concept that eternal life is a gift.

Why can we say that the above is incompatible with the concept of receiving a gift? That question is best answered by Anti-Nephi-Lehi. We read his words in Alma 24:11, *"And now behold, my brethren, since it has been all that we could do (as we were the most lost of all mankind) to repent of all our sins and the many murders which we have committed, and to get God to take them away from our hearts, for it was all we could do to repent sufficiently before God that he would take away our stain."* Anti-Nephi-Lehi trusted in the Lord and realized that all he could do was repent; there was not a long catalogue of deeds he cited as doing "all we can do." To the contrary, he realized that salvation lay solely in the merits, mercy, and grace of the Holy Messiah and it was all he could do to repent. Then in trusting the merits and mercy of the Savior, he realized His grace was sufficient for him and for his people. He received the gift.

EMBRACING HIM THROUGH FAITH

The plain fact is this: The Lord Jesus Christ has done all the work to create the gift of eternal life. Our works are not on par with His works, just as Lehi taught us above in 2 Nephi 2:8. It is the work of the Messiah that allows us to dwell in the presence of God, not our works. Accordingly, Nephi taught us in 2 Nephi 10:24, *"Wherefore, my beloved brethren, reconcile yourselves to the will of God, and not to the will of the devil and the flesh; and remember, after ye are reconciled unto God, that it is only in and through the grace of God that ye are saved."* Here Nephi does not add, "after all we can do." He realizes that we are saved by the work of the Savior and that our works reconcile us to God. Is that not what James taught us in James 2:22? Here we learn that our works make our faith perfect, not that they provide in any way salvation. We are reconciled to God when we accept His gift of salvation by accepting His grace through being born again. This means we reconcile ourselves to Him in faith, and only in faith can we receive His gift.

Consequently, when we read in our scriptures that Jesus Christ is in all things, it gives us a moment of pause to consider what that means. In Doctrine and Covenants 88:13, we read that He is *"The light which is in all things, which giveth life to all things, which is the law by which all things are governed, even the power of God who sitteth upon his throne, who is in the bosom of eternity, who is in the midst of all things."* The next verses tell us that each kingdom is governed by law, meaning the telestial kingdom is governed by telestial law; the terrestrial by terrestrial law; and the celestial kingdom is governed by celestial law. We must resist the temptation to think that celestial law is reduced to one of merits, awards and prizes, established by statute. If we do, we will be seeking for performance, so that we can exchange this performance for His work of salvation.

The law of the celestial kingdom is governed by the law of faith and by the love the Savior Himself established as the higher law (see John 15:12) where He said, *"This is my commandment: Love each other in the same way I have loved you"* (New Living Translation). What is that same way? It is to listen to His voice and then act as He would act. It is in being obedient to His commandments because we love Him, not because we seek to avoid punishment or to earn rewards.

Eternal life is not awarded to us, but is the incomprehensible gift of life due to the largess of the Savior. Accordingly, Lehi taught Jacob in 2 Nephi 2:3, *"Wherefore, I know that thou art redeemed, because of the righteousness of thy Redeemer..."* not because of our works, no matter how exquisite! What we need to do is to prepare ourselves to receive this gift. The Savior's love is not reduced to a catalogue of deeds, but because it is transformative, it re-orders our soul through the events known as being born again. This is how we receive the gift. The Savior made this clear in 3 Nephi 15:9 when he told us, *"Behold, I am the law, and the light. Look unto me, and endure to the end, and ye shall live; for unto him that endureth to the end will I give eternal life."* As a result, we now understand the meaning of living the celestial law. It is that we, as did Anti-Nephi-Lehi, realize that all we can do is bring forth the sacrifice of a broken heart and a contrite spirit and repent of our sins sufficiently that the Lord sends us the gift of faith which in turn allows His Spirit to justify and approve of our lives and our deeds. This occurs when we are born again to see and to enter His kingdom through the gate of baptism. This is why the Lord is both the law and the light. And if we endure to the end, we will receive His gift of eternal life. We now understand the meaning of Doctrine and Covenants 88:33, *"For what doth it profit a man if a gift is bestowed upon him, and he receive not the gift? Behold, he rejoices not in that which is given unto him, neither rejoices in him who is the giver of the gift."* This is what happens when we confuse a gift with an award. We are not awarded eternal life after all we can do—meaning we basically save ourselves—because this equates our works with His work. That is why we do not rejoice in the gift or in Him who is the giver of the gift of eternal life; instead we look to our works of compliance and through these works we seek to exalt ourselves.

The world rejoiced when baby Jessica was rescued; we rejoiced in the gift of life that the rescuers had bestowed on that child—and it wasn't because she had done anything to merit the gift. In fact, it could be said that she was careless and because she was, her deed caused her to fall into the well. All of that did not matter; we rejoiced in the gift and the givers of the gift. Our faith in God was strengthened that day. Why, we ask, is that so? It is because deep within the center of our soul we know that faith is also a gift. And this gift is a fundamental one, for without it, we cannot approach God nor can we receive anything from Him. In such a state, we rejoice not in His gifts because we esteem them as awards for our works and not for His. Faith is the gateway gift that allows us to embrace His gift of eternal life; because we receive faith as a gift, we will no longer seek to turn His gift into an award.

FAITH CENTERS OUR OBEDIENCE

Faith is a gift of the Spirit and is described as such by Paul in 1 Corinthians 12:9. It must therefore be clear that since it is a gift of the Spirit, and since we begin receiving gifts of the Spirit through sacrifice of things of the world, the ability to receive this gift of faith must come with sacrifice. This is a fundamental principle. We may have hope in Christ, but without sacrifice, we cannot receive the gift of redemptive faith. If we have hope in Christ, this means we believe in Him, but again, without sacrifice, the faith needed to access the power of God cannot happen. If we reject this premise, then we are "wise in our own eyes," and according to Proverbs 26:12, we have little hope for understanding our true interests. That is why the Lord has told us specifically in Doctrine and Covenants 59:8–9, *"Thou shalt offer a sacrifice unto the Lord thy God in righteousness, even that of a broken heart and a contrite spirit. And that thou mayest more fully keep thyself unspotted from the world..."*

The Lord warned us about this condition of "being wise in our own eyes" when He told us in Matthew 23:5, *"But all their works they do for to be seen of men: for they make broad their phylacteries, and enlarge the borders of their garments"*

(English Revised Version). Those who are not willing to sacrifice things of the self for the things of the soul do not really believe in God's promises. Thus they are acting against their true interests.

In today's world of ever increasing secularism where faith in Christ becomes a casualty, those who seek after the world and its rewards have become filled with vanity and pride. We must be ever vigilant in guarding our souls against this pernicious state of being because in such a state, we cannot receive the gift of faith, let alone the gift of eternal life. Moreover, Paul told us in Hebrews 11:6, *"And without faith it is impossible to be well-pleasing unto him: for he that cometh to God must believe that he is, and that he is a rewarder of them that seek after him"* (English Revised Version). This version of the Bible has a particularly good way of illustrating our point. We see that without faith, it is impossible to be well-pleasing to God, which means that obedience without faith is not well-pleasing, because such faithless obedience always has ulterior motives. These motives, like seeking to connect earthly blessings with obedience, betray our true interest and cause us to focus on vanity and, thereby, we contract the spiritual foot and mouth disease of Esau. Our worship becomes a form of vanity because we worship to be seen of men.

It is abundantly clear in all scripture that worship must include sacrifice to be worship. Because of this, what sometimes passes for worship is just a meeting of a service club. The Old Testament is filled with sacrifice. The New Testament chronicles the ultimate sacrifice of the Son of God. Do we think that if we seek for selfish rewards from God due to our obedience that it is truly sacrifice? No, such a motive for worship is used to bind God to our will rather than the other way around. Faith, then, is a gift of the Spirit given on condition of sacrifice. This is abundantly clear in the Old Testament after the Lord restored Judah from Babylon: over time the Jews fell into apostasy. Obedience became a sign of being favored in society as one who was pious, and hyper obedience led to privilege in that society.

This does not mean that we have *carte blanche* to disobey God's commandments, but it does mean the obedience we do render needs to be done because of our faith, for faith centers our obedience in Christ and our desire to be like Him. We saw in our example of Esau and Jacob that it was true that Esau, because he was loved by his father Isaac, kept the commandments. He simply did not have any faith, and therefore his obedience was not well-pleasing to God. It is also clear from scripture that Esau did not seek after the Lord but rather sought for the rewards of men. Pride ruled his heart to the extent that he valued the things of God as naught. He felt certain in his own gifts and thought matters of the soul were for the weak; he felt certain that Isaac would love him over Jacob, because he was a man "wise in his own eyes," and he esteemed himself above Jacob.

> **Faith centers our obedience in Christ and our desire to be like Him**

THE UNIVERSAL SIN

Pride, as a condition of the heart, is indeed the universal sin. President Ezra Taft Benson illustrated this point precisely in a landmark address to all, but particularly to any who wish to be considered disciples:

> Most of us think of pride as self-centeredness, conceit, boastfulness, arrogance, or haughtiness. All of these are elements of the sin, but the heart, or core, is still missing. The central feature of pride is enmity—enmity toward God and enmity toward our fellowmen. Enmity means "hatred toward, hostility to, or a state of opposition." It is the power by which Satan wishes to reign over us. Pride is essentially competitive in nature. We pit our will against God's. When we direct our pride toward God, it is in the spirit of "my will and not thine be done." As Paul said, they *"seek their own, not the things which are Jesus Christ's"* (Philippians 2:21). Our will in competition to God's will allows desires, appetites, and passions to go unbridled (see Alma 38:12; 3 Nephi 12:30). The proud cannot accept the authority of God giving direction to their lives (see Helaman 12:6).
>
> They pit their perceptions of truth against God's great knowledge, their abilities versus God's priesthood power, their accomplishments against His mighty works. Our enmity toward God takes on many labels, such as rebellion, hard-heartedness, stiff-neckedness, unrepentant, puffed up, easily offended, and sign seekers. The proud wish God to agree with them. They are not interested in changing their opinions to agree with God's. Another major portion of this very prevalent sin of pride is enmity toward our fellowmen. We are tempted daily to elevate ourselves above others and diminish them (see Helaman 6:17; Doctrine and Covenants 58:41). The proud make every man his adversary... ("Beware of Pride," *Ensign,* May 1989).

From President Benson's remarks we see why Alexander Solzhenitsyn was correct: pride is a condition of the heart. It is because the central feature of pride is enmity toward God and our fellowmen. Enmity is defined as a state of hostility toward someone or something. Esau is the poster child for such enmity. He was hostile toward God as he despised his birthright, and he was hostile toward Jacob, whom he felt was his inferior. It is our pride that causes us to win at all costs; it is our pride that seeks zealously the rewards of the world; and it is pride that causes us to be puffed up and extol our own abilities over those of our neighbors. Pride is truly a deadly sin, for it kills the soul and hardens the heart. The Lord has provided us a remedy to combat pride because pride is found in every man and woman as part of our mortal condition. That remedy is sacrifice. We saw that King Lamoni's father was willing to give up his kingdom to "see the kingdom of God" and be born again. And we have seen that we too must be humble so that we can "see the kingdom of God" and receive answers to our prayers. It is in humility that we begin the events that will re-order our soul to better reflect the subject of our faith, the Lord Jesus Christ and His light.

Our Savior identified this re-ordering of the soul as being born again, events that redirect our focus to the mission of the Savior. And as these events progress, we are to be baptized and receive the Holy Ghost. This is so we can be born of the water and of the spirit (John 3:5–10) and thus be able to enter the kingdom of God. It is through the gift of the Holy Ghost, accessed, according to Alma, by rejecting the temptation to glorify our own worth (Alma 36:5) and by partaking of the sacrament worthily, that we are able to "see the kingdom of God" and commence the events known as being born again. Then, as Oliver Cowdery learned (see Lesson Four), every time he would pray, his mind would be enlightened. So it is with us, too.

All of this now points us to the overall remedy that cures pride: the bringing forth of a broken heart and a contrite spirit. It is in this way that we overcome the natural man and put the affairs of the heart above those of the self. The scriptures are full of metaphors and examples as to why this is so important. For example, in the Old Testament, we learn that the animal sacrifice that was given under the Law of Moses needed to be given with a broken and contrite heart or it was not acceptable. We read in Psalms 51:16–17 and 19, *"For thou desirest not sacrifice; else would I give it: thou delightest not in burnt offering. The sacrifices of God are a broken spirit: a broken and a contrite heart, O God, thou wilt not despise.... Then shalt thou be pleased with the sacrifices of righteousness, with burnt offering and whole burnt offering: then shall they offer bullocks upon thine altar."* We have learned that if our obedience is offered so that we can earn a reward, our offering does not delight the Lord.

> **The overall remedy that cures pride: the bringing forth of a broken heart and a contrite spirit**

If we are being obedient so that our needs can be met—and not the needs the Savior wants for us—then we will not hear the Savior's call to us to be born again. We will not seek to re-order our soul to reflect His priorities and His traits of faith, virtue, and charity, because our own priorities—those that seek for a reward—take center stage. In fact, Lehi tells us without mincing any words why we must have a broken heart and a contrite spirit.

In 2 Nephi 2:7, we read, *"Behold, he offereth himself a sacrifice for sin, to answer the ends of the law, unto all those who have a broken heart and a contrite spirit; and unto none else can the ends of the law be answered."* Often, as young men and women, we are plagued by those who think they are better than we are. Those who think this certainly do not have a broken heart; they are vain and pride-filled and fall short of being true disciples.

RECEIVING THE SAVIOR WITH A BROKEN HEART

Because the gift of the Atonement is offered to us based upon our ability to bring forth a broken heart and a contrite spirit, once the events of being born again commence in our lives, we must continue and bring this sacrifice of our heart to the Lord. We must be meek and provide this sacrifice to Him to show our willingness to receive His gospel. And thus not only be born again of the Spirit to see the kingdom of God, but we must have a broken heart and a contrite spirit to enter the kingdom as well, even by baptism and confirmation. When we do this, He is then anxious to answer our prayers and open the libraries of heaven to us. He is anxious to accept our efforts at re-ordering our soul and sends confirmation to us by enlightening our minds as well as causing our hearts to swell with joy and peace—perhaps not so dramatically as He did with King Lamoni's father, but just as miraculously. And just as significantly, King Lamoni's father was willing to give up everything for this peace. Sacrifice is a vital part of worship as it shows our real intent and our willingness to do whatever the Lord wants us to do. We have repeatedly learned that we must be willing to sacrifice the things of the world for the things of the Spirit.

Sacrifice of the things of the world for the knowledge of heaven is often required when the events of being born again are prescient in our lives, but the sacrifice of a broken heart and a contrite spirit is always required if we wish to differentiate conformity to gospel principles from true obedience to gospel doctrines—true obedience allows our souls to be re-ordered in the image of Christ while conformity only changes our behavior temporarily. As we bring forth the sacrifice of a broken heart, the re-ordering of our soul commences. Of course our behavior will also change because we adopt the desires of the Lord.

If we pretend to change and fail to bring forth the broken heart, our behavior might change for a time; but, if we focus only on behavior modification, it is unclear that the desired re-ordering of our souls will ever begin. We read in Alma 32 that for the desired re-ordering to take place, we must be humble. In verses 16–18 we read, *"Therefore, blessed are they who humble themselves without being compelled to be humble… blessed is he that believeth in the word of God… without stubbornness of heart, yea, without being brought to know the word, or even compelled to know, before they will believe. Yea, there are many who do say: If thou wilt show unto us a sign from heaven… then we shall believe. Now I ask, is this faith? Behold, I say unto you, Nay.…"* If we are simply conforming to the commandments, we are being compelled to be humble since our obedience is only rendered because we are trying to avoid a punishment. It is better to be obedient in this conforming way than to not be obedient, but it is far better that we bring forth the sacrifice of the broken heart and the contrite spirit. For then the ends of the law can be answered on our behalf and we learn what it is to be meek.

The Savior's profound example of having a broken heart, as we learned in prior lessons, continues in His meekness. He served others even by the ultimate sacrifice of His precious life, because of His real intent and His willingness to do the will of the Father. We will realize the significance of making this sacrifice in quiet ways and in backwater places—what is more quiet or more intimate than the recesses of our heart? It is in this way that we will not be influenced by the world. Motives can be questioned in the world, especially if we seek good things selfishly; this is not the best motive. We most effectively practice Christianity at ground level, not at 30,000 feet! The poet reflects this sentiment (*Ensign,* May 1986, page 19):

> "Father, where shall I work today?"
> And my love flowed warm and free.
> Then He pointed a tiny spot
> And said, "Tend that for me."
> I answered quickly, "Oh no, not that!
> Then no one would ever see,
> No matter how well my work was done,
> Not that little place for me."
> And the word He spoke, it was not stern,
> He answered tenderly:
> "Ah, little one, search that heart of thine,
> Art thou working for them or for me?
> Nazareth was a little place,
> And so was Galilee."

THE PERSUASIVE POWER OF MEEKNESS

Do we not see that the work of softening the heart is done in the intimate recesses of the soul? After all, since pride is a condition of the heart, so is meekness. Meekness conveys the power of Christ in ways that bespeak deep faith in Christ. We read of Moses, who was a dispensation head like Joseph Smith, that he was a great example of meekness as well as a man of great faith who wrought miracles by his faith. In Numbers 12:3 we read, *"Now the man Moses was very meek, above all the men which were upon the face of the earth."* It is within the heart, therefore, that we find meekness. It is in this meek condition, brought about by a broken heart and a contrite spirit that the elements of faith come together. It is then with faith, a gift of God to a meek soul, that we make sacrifices for that faith. This does not occur because of the self, for the self only wants rewards and seeks not for the things of the soul. We make sacrifices of the things of the world as a necessary effort to accept the Atonement of the Savior. We then willingly accept His grace and His gifts of repentance and rebirth so that we might be joint heirs with Him in the kingdom of His Father. We read in Romans 8:17, *"And if children, then heirs; heirs of God, and joint-heirs with Christ; if so be that we suffer with him, that we may be also glorified together."* We suffer with Him when we sacrifice for Him.

We sacrifice when we bring forth the broken heart and the contrite spirit so that we can put off the natural man and seek for a relationship with things eternal over our desire for earthly gain and worldly success. When we bring the broken heart and the contrite spirit to the Lord, He in turn acknowledges this sacrifice by giving us the gift of faith and by pouring His Spirit into our lives. Without sacrifice, even that of a broken heart and a contrite spirit, there can be no worship. We can only worship if there is sacrifice, for without it we cannot be kept unspotted from the world. We have read previously where King David taught in Psalms 51:17 and 19 that before we make the necessary physical sacrifice, we need to have a broken heart; the reason for this is that the worship of Israel was not pleasing to God without such a sacrifice. Thus, without sacrifice, even of a broken heart and a contrite spirit, the Lord cannot keep us unspotted from the world.

The Lord further confirms these desires of those who have a broken heart and a contrite spirit by sending the Holy Ghost to enlighten our minds with hope for these desires. If we are not yet baptized, then we must be open to see the kingdom of God by being born of the Spirit; then we will be prepared to enter the kingdom of God because we have indeed been blessed with the ability to see His kingdom. We read in Doctrine and Covenants 20:37, *"And again, by way of commandment to the church concerning the manner of baptism—All those who humble themselves before God, and desire to be baptized, and come forth with broken hearts and contrite spirits, and witness before the church that they have truly repented of all their sins, and are willing to take upon them the name of Jesus Christ... shall be received by baptism into his church."*

We can now be baptized and have the Holy Ghost remit our sins even with fire (see 2 Nephi 31:17), and if we already have been baptized, then the Holy Ghost will renew our faith and enlighten our minds with refreshingly new vision (again, see Doctrine and Covenants 6:14–15). Our prayers find answers and we continue to be born again. With a broken heart and a contrite spirit—the building blocks of faith—we possess the power to not be disbelieved. We read in 3 Nephi 7:18, *"... they were angry with him, even because he had greater power than they, for it were not possible that they could disbelieve his words, for so great was his faith on the Lord Jesus Christ that angels did minister unto him daily."*

JUSTIFIED BY THE SAVIOR THROUGH THE SPIRIT

Lehi taught the following in 2 Nephi 2:5, *"And men are instructed sufficiently that they know good from evil. And the law is given unto men. And by the law no flesh is justified…"* In verse 7, Lehi tells us why this is so, *"Behold, he offereth himself a sacrifice for sin, to answer the ends of the law, unto all those who have a broken heart and a contrite spirit; and unto none else can the ends of the law be answered."* We are justified not by the law, nor even by unsighted obedience. We are justified by our Savior, through the Spirit, when we are born again. We are born again, as the Savior taught Nicodemus, by first being able to see His kingdom through a broken heart and a contrite spirit—the conditions that allow us to accept the gift of faith and sight—and then to enter His kingdom by water, through baptism.

Without meekness presented by the broken heart, we cannot have faith, and without faith, as we learned above, we are not well-pleasing to God. Then, our obedience is undertaken for less than virtuous reasons. Without a broken heart or a contrite spirit, our obedience comes only so that we can earn rewards or to avoid punishments. When we seek to "buy off the Lord through obedience," can we not now see that we really are immersed in the world? We certainly are not keeping ourselves unspotted from the world, and in fact have become "wise in our own eyes"—the very condition that defines pride (Proverbs 26:12). Is this not the way of the world, to be cunning and lucky?

Being born again to see the kingdom of God and then making the sacrifice of a broken heart and a contrite spirit let us enter the kingdom with vigor. We make this sacrifice privately and personally, never in a public setting to be seen of men (see again Matthew 6). We read in Matthew 4:1 of the time Jesus went into the wilderness. In the Joseph Smith Translation, the verse reads, *"Then was Jesus led up of the Spirit into the wilderness to be with God."* He wasn't led into the wilderness to be tempted of the devil, but Satan came to Him while He was there. It was while He was in the wilderness in a very private setting that He committed His soul to do the will of the Father. We read in verses 2–9 that the things of the world were presented to Him, and in verse 9, the devil said, *"All these things will I give thee, if thou wilt fall down and worship me."*

Is this not the promise of the world? Is this not always the entreaty that causes us to be the natural man, filled with pride and vanity? Many of us lust after the things of the world and labor assiduously to gain them. The Savior's response in verse 10 sums up why we must be born again, why we must have a broken heart and a contrite spirit, *"Begone, Satan! Jesus replied; for it is written, 'To the Lord thy God thou shalt do homage, and to Him alone shalt thou render worship'"* (Weymouth New Testament). It is clear: by bringing forth the broken heart and the contrite spirit we are telling Satan to be gone! That does not mean he will refrain from pestering us, but it does signal our willingness for this not to be; it does show we are willing to do as King Benjamin asked of us when we want to repudiate the natural man.

QUESTIONS ABOUT THE LESSON

01
Why are gifts different from awards and why does the Lord prefer gifts?

02
How do we receive the gift of faith?

03
How do we access the redemptive power of the Lord?

04
Why do we need to be careful not to find God's acceptance of our sacrifice in the rewards of the world?

05
How does meekness give us power over Satan?

07

INCREASING OUR FAITH

We have learned that faith is a gift given to us as we bring forth a broken heart and a contrite spirit. We have seen how faith is made redemptive when it is combined with love. Then, as we receive the gift of faith, we begin to see the kingdom of God, which initiates the events known as being born again. In the course of these events, it is then that faith transcends its definition as a principle, which of course it is, and becomes a law. It is the law of faith that allows us to have power in our faith. As we continue to experience the events of spiritual rebirth, our faith begins to be unshakeable (see Enos 1:11 and 15). Such a person desires to enter and grow in the attributes that pertain to the kingdom of God—attributes like faith, hope and charity—so that the image of Christ can be engraved in their souls.

To that end, Peter lays out attributes that come because we have faith, hope, and charity. In 2 Peter 1:4–8 we read, *"Whereby are given unto us exceeding great and precious promises: that by these ye might be partakers of the divine nature, having escaped the corruption that is in the world through lust. And beside this, giving all diligence, add to your faith virtue; and to virtue knowledge; And to knowledge temperance; and to temperance patience; and to patience godliness; And to godliness brotherly kindness; and to brotherly kindness charity. For if these things be in you, and abound, they make you that ye shall neither be barren nor unfruitful in the knowledge of our Lord Jesus Christ."* You see, as we increase our faith, these things like virtue, knowledge, and charity will be added upon. Thus, as our faith becomes redemptive faith, clothed with hope and love, it grows. It is then able to add these traits to it, including charity, which is the pure love of Christ.

As we desire these things that Peter identified as traits that make us "fruitful in the knowledge of our Lord Jesus Christ," we see that life is beset with a range of events that bring us happiness, but also events that require sacrifice and events that cause us to suffer. These attributes Peter identified can be found in us as we change and re-order our souls, if we experience these things as the events of spiritual rebirth. Needless to say, this is a life-long journey. The fact that all lives experience the vicissitudes of mortality is a fact of life; but as we learn to improve our state of being through faith, even by the things we must sacrifice and the things that cause us suffering, these then give us discipline. They cause us to repent and change; they make us holy, not haughty. Paul taught this in Hebrews 12:2 and 7. Here we read, "... *simply fixing our gaze upon Jesus, our Prince Leader in the faith, who will also award us the prize. He, for the sake of the joy which lay before Him, patiently endured the cross, looking with contempt upon its shame, and afterwards seated Himself—where He still sits—at the right hand of the throne of God.... The sufferings that you are enduring are for your discipline. God is dealing with you as sons; for what son is there whom his father does not discipline"* (Weymouth New Testament).

Paul then continues and tells us why we must be disciplined to be born again. In verses 8–10 we read, *"Furthermore we have had fathers of our flesh which corrected us, and we gave them reverence: shall we not much rather be in subjection unto the Father of spirits, and live? But if ye be without chastisement, whereof all are partakers, then are ye bastards, and not sons. For they verily for a few days chastened us ... but he for our profit, that we might be partakers of his holiness."* All of the examples we have used in these lessons show sacrifice and suffering. All of the people who were highlighted saw their souls re-ordered. They were fortified with virtue and love, hope, and charity. They exemplified the admonition of Paul found in Hebrews 12. In order for them to experience these events known as being born again, they had to learn to increase their faith. And now, so must we.

THE UNPROFITABLE SERVANT

This brings us to the central point of this lesson: how do we increase our faith? The apostles came to the Savior and asked Him this very question. An account of what He taught is given in Luke, chapter 17:5–10, where we read the Lord's answer as to how we increase our faith, *"And the apostles said unto the Lord, Increase our faith. And the Lord said, If ye had faith as a grain of mustard seed, ye might say unto this sycamine tree, Be thou plucked up by the root, and be thou planted in the sea; and it should obey you."*

Alright, so far so good. Now the Savior gives us the key to increasing our faith: *"But which of you, having a servant plowing or feeding cattle, will say unto him by and by, when he is come from the field, Go and sit down to meat? And will not rather say unto him, Make ready wherewith I may sup, and gird thyself, and serve me, till I have eaten and drunken; and afterward thou shalt eat and drink? Doth he thank that servant because he did the things that were commanded him? I trow not. So likewise ye, when ye shall have done all those things which are commanded of you, say, We are unprofitable servants: we have done that which was our duty to do."*

It is clear that the relationship between obedience and faith is established when we do all that we are commanded to do and yet do not think we have earned our blessings. Even after we have proved to be obedient, we are yet unprofitable servants. Consider the example of Mother Teresa. She never exalted herself; but rather, always considered herself to be an unprofitable servant. She always thought more about those she served than she did about herself. She never thought she had "earned" her reward; but showed us that it is by works that our faith is made perfect, not the other way around. We are not made perfect in our works, but because our works are never perfect, we continue to view ourselves as unprofitable servants. We see that it is our faith that is made perfect by our works, not that our works are made perfect by our faith. We are made perfect by our Savior and not by our works. Remember, it was because of his great faith that Nephi's brethren could not disbelieve his words, not because of his works (3 Nephi 7:18). We remain the unprofitable servant even after we have done all we can do, and this for good reason.

We know that it is only through faith that we are well pleasing to God, and should our works supplant our faith to make us so, we would in fact become prideful and vain servants, and think that we, through our obedience, have brought into existence our own salvation. In this state of mind, we arrogantly thank the Lord for His sacrifice, but then focus on our own "greatness and glory" for being wise enough to be perfectly obedient. This is folly and the Lord responded to this kind of thinking by asking, "Does he thank the servant for doing those things that were commanded of him? I don't think so." Faith is increased by our obedience, but it doesn't come by obedience. Just like our obedience is not the author of our faith—the author is Jesus Christ, who gives us faith through the Holy Ghost as we bring forth a broken heart and a contrite spirit. We do know, however, that obedience is required to make our faith perfect.

It is from this condition of vanity and pride that Mother Teresa did not suffer. As we will yet see, it was the humble men and women among the great leaders who appeared to Wilford Woodruff in the St. George Temple. They were humbled by the work of the Savior and they had accepted His work, sought His grace as they repented of their sins, and now were in a position to enter into a covenant with Him so that they might be saved. As we have declared throughout these lessons, faith and repentance always lead us to seek the saving ordinances of baptism and confirmation, either in this life or the next, for baptism is the gateway to salvation and exaltation.

We have learned in these examples thus far, that if we are obedient in faith, that it is this sighted obedience that always leads us to desire to participate in ordinances. It is through the ordinances of the gospel, as they are empowered by our faith, that the blessings of heaven are sealed upon the heads of the Lord's children. A key to coming to know this, as well as to increase our faith, comes to us as we continue in bringing forth the broken heart and the contrite spirit as evidenced by thinking of ourselves as unprofitable servants. Paul taught us in Romans 3:10–12, *"As it is written, There is none righteous, no, not one: There is none that understandeth, there is none that seeketh after God. They are all gone out of the way, they are together become unprofitable; there is none that doeth good, no, not one."* There it is again, the idea that even though we are obedient, we are yet unprofitable, even unprofitable servants. We must ever view ourselves, even in our obedience, as unprofitable servants.

We know that it is the Lord and His sacrifice that makes salvation and exaltation possible; it is the Lord's work and only through the "merits, and mercy, and grace of the holy Messiah" (2 Nephi 2:8), that salvation and exaltation come into being; indeed, not through our works are we saved. And as He is the One who brings salvation and exaltation to pass in the lives of we who dwell in mortality, we must seek Him in faith and not through our works.

HIS TRUTH ILLUMINATES OUR SOUL

King Benjamin provides additional context to the fact that when we are unprofitable servants, our faith is made perfect. We read in Mosiah 2:20–21, *"I say unto you, my brethren, that if you should render all the thanks and praise which your whole soul has power to possess, to that God who has created you, and has kept and preserved you, and has caused that ye should rejoice, and has granted that ye should live in peace one with another—I say unto you that if ye should serve him who has created you from the beginning, and is preserving you from day to day, by lending you breath, that ye may live and move and do according to your own will, and even supporting you from one moment to another—I say, if ye should serve him with all your whole souls yet ye would be unprofitable servants."*

We learn from King Benjamin that whatever action we take, we must understand completely the correct foundation that this action is only made possible because our Lord has allowed it, and because of this, we must give thanks and praise to Him who preserved us. In that way, we continue to recognize our condition as unprofitable servants. There is no arrogance here, nor is there any thought that our actions produce salvation. With this understanding in place, King Benjamin tells us in verse 23 that when we view ourselves as unprofitable servants, all the Lord then requires of us is that we keep His commandments.

King Benjamin then continues to explain in verses 23–25 how our keeping of the commandments will increase our faith once we acknowledge we are unprofitable servants: *"And now, in the first place, he hath created you, and granted unto you your lives, for which ye are indebted unto him. And secondly, he doth require that ye should do as he hath commanded you; for which if ye do, he doth immediately bless you; and therefore he hath paid you. And ye are still indebted unto him, and are, and will be, forever and ever; therefore, of what have ye to boast? And now I ask, can ye say aught of yourselves? I answer you, Nay. Ye cannot say that ye are even as much as the dust of the earth...but behold, it belongeth to him who created you."*

Are we beginning to get the point? As we accept His work of salvation and exaltation, just as Peter told us above, we

> **Our works make our faith perfect only if they are done for the love of the Savior**

long for baptism. We long to receive the gift of the Holy Ghost so that we can receive the gift of redemptive faith. With that gift, we seek in perpetuity to be His unprofitable servant, laboring in His service to bring the knowledge of His work to the world. In that way, our faith is increased. Our works make our faith perfect only if they are done for the love of the Savior. Faith is never increased by boasting of our goodness or by our works; rather, we rejoice as His truth illuminates our own soul and the souls of those with whom we labor. This becomes our great joy—to be a servant of the most High and a servant to His people. In this way, we love our Savior as He has loved us. In this way we are obedient to the new commandment, to love as Jesus loved (John 13:54).

THE EXAMPLE OF THE SONS OF MOSIAH

Once again we see how the example of the sons of Mosiah teach us about being a suffering servant, and truly being unprofitable servants, as they took the teachings of King Benjamin to heart. We read in Alma 17 of Ammon's response to King Lamoni, when asked why he was there among the Lamanites. We read in Alma 17:22–23 and 25, *"And the king inquired of Ammon if it were his desire to dwell in the land among the Lamanites, or among his people. And Ammon said unto him: Yea, I desire to dwell among this people for a time; yea, and perhaps until the day I die."* The king was so pleased that he offered Ammon one of his daughters as a wife, but Ammon declined and re-emphasized the reason he was there by saying, *"But Ammon said unto him: Nay, but I will be thy servant."* By our ability to recognize the need to be a servant, even an unprofitable servant of God, we recognize that our Savior is our Lord and we honor His sacrifice for us and our love for Him when we seek to be His servant. Then, our faith will increase; we will never think our obedience will earn our salvation, but we will seek for redemptive faith so that His will can be accomplished. Only in faith can we be well-pleasing to God. We then realize that our ability to do the works He has commanded us to do enhances our faith. As we accept His gift of salvation and exaltation by being baptized and by receiving His other gifts, then, by our works, our faith will be made perfect.

As we learn to be an "unprofitable servant" we do not understand this to mean that our service is unprofitable. Indeed, we see that this term is meant to instill in us one fundamental and indisputable fact: the Lord's work and His Atonement are so much greater than our works that we should never boast, nor should we ever equate our works with His works. If we learn this lesson our faith will increase. If we feel our works are on the same level as His works, our faith will not increase, but over time will become clouded and ineffective. This is why Alma told us in the last lesson, and it bears repeating again, *"And see that ye have faith, hope, and charity, and then ye will always abound in good works"* (Alma 7:24). This is again consistent with our understanding that faith must come first, before obedience. Since faith is a gift, given to us when we bring forth the broken heart and the contrite spirit, it cannot increase if we invert our understanding. We must know that obedience, while absolutely necessary, did not create our faith. If we have faith first, along with hope and charity, then we will always abound in good works and our faith will then increase as our ability to receive truth from the Holy Ghost also increases.

With the understanding that our faith must come first, we will be unprofitable servants because we will bring forth the sacrifice of a broken heart and a contrite spirit. Then our love for the Savior will increase as well as our faith, and in that way, our faith will indeed be made perfect in our works. This is just as James tells in his epistle cited above. If we invert our understanding and seek to obtain faith through our works, then our faith will remain mere belief, and it certainly will not increase. Instead, this belief will never become redemptive faith and might ultimately collapse. Since the superstructure of faith will have never been built, because obedience will have been rendered before we have faith, we will easily be lead into prideful thinking as we feel we are profitable servants—such preliminary faith will eventually be discarded and dismissed as we seek for empirical evidence for our belief.

We read in Alma 32:34–36 about the knowledge we obtain through faith, *"And now, behold, is your knowledge perfect? Yea, your knowledge is perfect in that thing, and your faith is dormant; and this because you know, for ye know that the word hath swelled your souls, and ye also know that it hath sprouted up, that your understanding doth begin to be enlightened, and your mind doth begin to expand. O then, is this not real? I say unto you, Yea, because it is light; and whatsoever is light, is good, because it is discernible, therefore ye must know that it is good; and now behold, after ye have tasted this light is your knowledge perfect? Behold I say unto you, Nay; neither must ye lay aside your faith...."* If we were to "lay aside our faith," our knowledge of spiritual things would collapse. If we fail to continue to follow the law of faith, any knowledge obtained by that law will leave us and we will be confused. We are then subject to being side-lined with crippling doubt, which disables our knowledge obtained through faith.

THE CONSEQUENCE OF A PRIDEFUL HEART

We learned previously that Oliver Cowdery was born again in faith, and as these events began in his life, his heart was softened and he received answers to his prayers. His example was a model for us as we would seek answers regarding service as a disciple. But Oliver lost his faith and the swelling of his heart and soul ceased when he no longer trusted God and instead looked to his own abilities; he became prideful and thought his works to be the works of God. If we put our trust in our works first, the word of God does not swell our hearts; instead, the substance that we find is not a well-grounded assurance—a conviction of the reality of things which we do not see—instead, it is pride.

George Washington provides a counterpoint to Oliver Cowdery. He knew that he needed to trust God and so he did not think his abilities to be superior; he remained the suffering and unprofitable servant. He knew that faith must come first, then obedience. With this sequence in mind, he found that his works gave him vision, which in turn strengthened his faith. If faith is first, then knowledge becomes certain just as we learned previously with Oliver Cowdery. He was taught in Doctrine and Covenants 6:14–15 that it was his mind that would be enlightened every time he prayed. He was then exhorted in verse 20 to be faithful—meaning full of faith—when keeping the commandments of God. We read, *"Behold, thou art Oliver, and I have spoken unto thee because of thy desires; therefore treasure up these words in thy heart. Be faithful and diligent in keeping the commandments of God, and I will encircle thee in the arms of my love."*

It was then that Oliver's faith began to be redemptive; it was then that his soul was filled with light and the superstructure of his faith began to bear fruit; it was then that his knowledge began to expand as his mind and his heart was enlightened. This knowledge, grounded in his faith, led his faith to become dormant, but it remained the very foundation of this spiritual knowledge. Unfortunately, it was at this time that he also began to be filled with pride. He laid his faith aside and relied heavily on his own abilities. His mighty works became the primary focus of his knowledge. The events of being born again had commenced in his soul. However, due to the challenging events that surrounded him, Oliver did not nourish his faith. His faith therefore failed and he became overcome with pride. He began to see Joseph Smith as a fallen prophet and thought, just because he was with Joseph at some of the most memorable events of the restoration, that he should be considered equal with Joseph.

When this happens to us, as it did in the case of Oliver Cowdery, we no longer possess a broken heart nor a contrite spirit. The knowledge of God that was expanding in our hearts begins to die. Our faith, the very substance that drives the events of being born again, ceases and our rebirth is stillborn. On the other hand, if we put works first and find our hearts filled with pride, then our nascent faith never grows to be redemptive faith—instead of becoming a superstructure upon which our knowledge can be sustained, pride eats away at our faith and then, rather than becoming dormant, it instead putrefies and dies. We are left bereft of faith and then, as we have also learned, our works are no longer pleasing to God. Happily, Oliver recovered his faith. In the ten years he was away from the Church, he began to view himself as an unprofitable servant again. As his faith returned, he sought to be re-baptized and to once again make everlasting covenants with the Lord. He worked with Phineas Young, Brigham Young's brother, to recover those things most precious to him, which were lost because of pride (see "The Return of Oliver Cowdery," *Oliver Cowdery—Scribe, Elder, Witness,* page 331).

The Savior taught this poignantly in Matthew 7:22–23, *"Many will say to me in that day, Lord, Lord, have we not prophesied in thy name? and in thy name have cast out devils? and in thy name done many wonderful works? And then will I profess unto them, I never knew you: depart from me, ye that work iniquity."* In the Weymouth New Testament, verse 23 is rendered, *"And then I will tell them plainly, 'I never knew you: begone from me you doers of wickedness.'"* In this translation, the Lord, clearly moved unfavorably if we do works without faith, calls those who have actually driven out devils, even prophesied in his name, as well as those who point to their "wonderful works," doers of wickedness. Why? Is it because those who consider their works wonderful truly embody pride, the complete antithesis of being an unprofitable servant? We know that without faith it is not possible to be well-pleasing to God, and so our works, done without faith, fail because the superstructure of faith Alma describes is no longer in place. Our spiritual knowledge turns to darkness and we are found bereft of the Spirit and the light of Christ is not found within us.

QUESTIONS ABOUT THE LESSON

01
How do we increase our faith?

02
Why do we need to consider ourselves unprofitable servants?

03
How do I receive redemptive faith, and how is redemptive faith different from non-redemptive faith?

04
Why do faith and the love of the Savior lead us to embrace charity?

05
Why will my ability to receive truth from the Holy Ghost increase?

08

FAITH AND VIRTUE

The scriptures are filled with stories about men and women of faith. As we read of them, we seem to drift from our present world and enter a world that once was—a world of men and women of faith that seems to no longer exist. If it were to exist, we opine, those persons of faith wouldn't do very well; to us they would appear to live in a dream world divorced from the "real world" of facts and numbers. As we seek relevance for today for men and women of faith, we often seek in vain. In today's society faith has frequently been replaced with science. We use behavior modification very successfully as we arm ourselves with day-planners, goal-setting programs, and efficiency-driven performance models, all of which are designed to make us better. We must admit, when we undertake the use of these things, we are made better. With that said however, if we look closely, we would find episodes of faith that defy science occurring every day. Prayers are answered, souls are changed and people are born again by the Spirit as they seek faith through a broken heart and a contrite spirit.

In our day, faith seems rather medieval—to be legitimate, we think it must be rationalized to some sort of behavior that involves "doing something." Whether it is by adopting principles of behavior modification or undertaking "steps to success" that are designed to make our faith less otherworldly, we seek for ways to make faith more scientific in the belief that faith will become easier to understand. While this may appear to be true, what is then taken for faith is not faith. It is stylized belief, which is good, but the substance known as faith has fled. Paul gives us a great definition of faith in Hebrews 11:1. In the Weymouth New Testament, this verse reads, *"Now faith is a well-grounded assurance of that for which we hope, and a conviction of the reality of things which we do not see."* As we look at this definition, it is readily apparent that science, the way we learn things through our senses, has no application when it comes to understanding faith. We note with confidence then, that faith is a well-grounded assurance—meaning we have received the assurance from realms outside science—of the truthfulness of real things that we do not see.

FAITH IS BOTH A LAW AND PRINCIPLE

We have learned in the previous lesson that faith comes to us as a gift, given when we bring forth a broken heart and a contrite spirit. We have further learned that we must love as the Savior loved, for this too is a commandment. An example of this love was manifested by the Savior with respect to the washing of the feet. So it is, as the Savior demonstrated, that by the sacrifice of the self in humility with no thought of personal gain, the soul is nourished. As a result of this sacrifice through the gift of selfless love, faith is made redemptive by love. When we have received this love as the gift of charity, we then realize that faith is both a principle and a law. This happens when our faith is mixed with charity; it becomes redemptive faith, filled with power and vision. Such faith is also virtuous and causes us to seek after virtue, not merely to ask, "Is what I am doing right?" We now have a higher standard: to do those things that are virtuous.

Consequently, when we try to make faith into a science experiment, we often do not find faith; although we may find truth, it has not been obtained by faith. Children have the purest faith, but as they grow older, it is too often replaced by principles of rational thought that are often perceived to be more sophisticated. Faith is often not rational—that does not mean it is irrational—but its substance comes from God and is not found by adopting the scientific method of truth's discovery. As we have so often made clear, faith is a gift given by God to the broken hearted. Faith is always a characteristic of virtue. People who embrace Christian virtue look to faith as the prime motivator for their actions; people of faith always embrace virtue as a prized attribute, because they also love the Lord, the redeemer of the soul. They also embrace faith as a law. We read in Jeremiah 31:31–33, *"Behold, the days come, saith the Lord, that I will make a new covenant with the house of Israel, and with the house of Judah: Not according to the covenant that I made with their fathers in the day that I took them by the hand to take them out of the land of Egypt… But this shall be the covenant that I will make with the house of Israel; After those days, saith the Lord, I will put my law in their inward parts, and write it in their hearts; and will be their God, and they shall be my people."*

Jeremiah told us that faith and love will be fused together as a new commandment, to love each other in that same way that Jesus loved us (John 15:12). A new covenant which establishes faith not only as a principle found in the realms where spiritual truth is taught, but it now becomes a law by which the covenant people must live. This is the law the Lord will put "in their inward parts" and write "in their hearts:" the law of faith. Paul amplifies this understanding of faith as a law in his letter to the Corinthians. We read, *"Such is the confidence which we have through Christ in the presence of God; not that of ourselves we are competent to decide anything by our own reasonings, but our competency comes from God. It is He also who has made us competent to serve Him in connexion with a new Covenant, which is not a written code but a Spirit; for the written code inflicts death, but the Spirit gives life"* (2 Corinthians 3:4–6, Weymouth New Testament).

It is in this context of faith as a law that Paul explained Jeremiah's words to the Saints of his times in Hebrews 8:10–11, *"But this is the Covenant that I will covenant with the house of Israel after those days, says the Lord: I will put My laws into their minds and will write them upon their hearts. And I will indeed be their God and they shall be My People. And there shall be no need for them to teach each one his fellow citizen and each one his brother, saying, Know the Lord. For all will know Me from the least of them to the greatest"* (Weymouth New Testament). We cited Paul in Ephesians 5:2 to support this view and it bears repeating now. We read that when we have made sacrifices to obtain faith and receive the gift of charity, the pure love of Christ, we live with virtue, *"And live and act lovingly, as Christ also loved you and gave Himself up to death on our behalf as an offering and sacrifice to God…"* (Weymouth New Testament). As we recognize faith as both a principle and a law, we seek after virtue. This is why Jesus responded the way He did when the edge of His garment was touched, *"And Jesus said, Somebody hath touched me: for I perceive that virtue is gone out of me"* (Luke 8:46). We read Luke 8:46 differently in the Weymouth New Testament: *"Some one has touched me," Jesus replied, "for I feel that power has gone from me."*

What we learn from these two translations is simply this: virtue is power and both of these attributes are governed by faith. This leads to an understanding that faith is a law as well as a principle. It is by understanding faith as a law as well as a principle that we initiate the events known as being born again. This means that we must learn to see by faith; we must look beyond the physical world around us to that world where the Holy Ghost becomes our guide and teacher. Thus, being born of the Spirit (see John 3:3–7 and Mosiah 27:25–27) becomes our goal as a disciple of Christ. As these events commence, we feel our hearts and souls being re-ordered so that the Savior's desire that we be one with Him through the Father's name (John 17:11) can be realized.

Peter explained the close relationship between faith, virtue, and knowledge obtained by faith in 2 Peter 1:5, *"For this very reason, make every effort to supplement your faith with virtue, and virtue with knowledge"* (English Standard Version). Because character follows virtue, if we are not virtuous, our character is less than what it could be. When we are able to make our faith redemptive faith by bringing forth the dual sacrifices of a broken heart and a contrite spirit, along with the sacrifice

> **We are sacrificing those things that gratify the self for those that feed the soul**

of the suffering servant—in the way Christ did when He washed the feet of the Twelve—this dual sacrifice produces virtue and virtue produces power! Because of this, it is clear that the sacrifice we make to be virtuous is that same sacrifice required for faith, even that of bringing forth a broken heart. We are sacrificing those things that gratify the self for those that feed the soul.

GEORGE WASHINGTON'S EXAMPLE

The following true story of the American Revolution is particularly poignant and illustrates how faith is indeed an unseen assurance that reflects a reality, or substance, that is not seen but is pivotal to the outcome. This unseen faith was further assured by the virtue of George Washington. He is a most acute example of a great leader who relied on his faith, which continued to grow even as events overtook him. George Washington's faith was showcased at the Battle of Trenton in December 1776. The following account has been abridged by the author:

> George Washington, earlier in 1776, had been defeated in the numerous battles for New York City. His army had been shattered and its remnants had crossed into New Jersey in late fall of 1776, vigorously pursued by the British. Washington sought the protection provided by the barrier of the Delaware River. As they retreated, Washington faced an additional crisis: at the end of 1776, much of his remaining Army was set to evaporate through expiring enlistments. Many of his soldiers were on track to go home. Badly

reduced, the Continental Army was poorly supplied and ill-equipped for winter with many of the men still in summer uniforms or lacking shoes. In a stroke of luck, the British commander ordered a halt to the pursuit on December 14th, and directed his army to enter their winter encampment. In so doing, they established a series of outposts across northern New Jersey. Consolidating his forces in Pennsylvania on December 20th, Washington was reinforced by around 2,700 men.... With the morale of the army and the public both ebbing, Washington believed that a daring act was required to restore confidence.

Meeting with his officers, he proposed a bold surprise attack on the Hessian garrison at Trenton for December 26th. For the operation, he intended to cross the Delaware River with 2,400 men and march south against the town. General James Ewing and 700 Pennsylvania militiamen were to cross at Trenton and seize the bridge over Assunpink Creek to prevent enemy troops from escaping. Combating rain, sleet, and snow, Washington's army reached the river at McConkey's Ferry on the evening of December 25th. Behind schedule, they were ferried across the ice-choked river by Colonel John Glover's Marblehead regiment. Glover had previously saved Washington's army from annihilation in New York. Behind schedule, the army had been ferried across by 3:00 AM. They then began their march toward Trenton. Sending out advance parties, the army moved south together until reaching Birmingham. Here General Nathanael Green's division turned inland to attack Trenton from the north.

Both columns approached the outskirts of Trenton shortly before 8:00 AM on December 26th. Driving in the Hessian pickets, Green's men opened the attack and drew enemy troops north from the river road. While Greene's men blocked the escape routes to Princeton, Henry Knox's artillery were deployed at the heads of the streets that would be used for escape. As the Americans attacked, Colonel Johann Rall, the Hessian commander, attempted to rally his troops. Knox's cannon prevented the Hessians from forming into lines. Heavy fire from General Hugh Mercer's brigade caused Rall to fall back.... American firepower blocked the assault and a sharpshooter's bullet put an end to Rall's life. The Hessians took heavy losses.

Driving the enemy back into a nearby orchard, Washington surrounded the survivors and forced their surrender. In the operation against Trenton, 22 Hessians were killed, 83 wounded, and 896 captured. The Americans suffered only two deaths...five wounded, including a near-fatal wound to future President James Monroe. Though a minor engagement...the victory at Trenton had a massive effect on the colonial war effort. Instilling a new confidence in the army at the Continental Congress, the triumph at Trenton boosted public morale and increased enlistments (*George Washington, A Biography,* pages 141–147).

The victory also showcased Washington's faith in God and his ability to lead others to find their faith, even to increase it. When the casualties were counted, and only two had died, Washington was overcome. He knelt in prayer and gave thanks to Almighty God for his deliverance. When he asked why so few had died, paraphrasing Hugh Mercer, who himself would die in battle in the not too distant future, was reported to have said, "General, these men fought for you because they love you; they would never dishonor the trust you placed in them" (see *Washington's Crossing,* pages 375–379 and *George Washington:*

The Crossing, page 58). Is it not clear that faith, linked to love and virtue, creates a power that is beyond the measurement of the senses; a power unavailable to the secular world?

Washington was indeed a suffering servant; he viewed himself even as an unprofitable servant, one fully dependent on God's grace. He thanked our Heavenly Father for the plan, but he relied fully on God's power to deliver the victory, for on paper, his army was no match for the Hessians. Do we not see how love, faith, and virtue mix together to create powerful leadership in similitude to the leadership of the Savior? Washington's men loved him because he loved them and sacrificed for them. His entire life attests to this love and this faith; he lived virtuously his entire life!

LINKING VIRTUE WITH FAITH

In this example, we uncover a fundamental truth: when we are virtuous, we seek to increase our faith. We also come to love God with such virtue and this then creates power in the soul. As such, we see ourselves as unprofitable servants, and because we have a virtuous heart, one that rises above self-interest, we prize the development of our faith.

> **When we are virtuous, we seek to increase our faith**

The author has visited the grave of Colonel Johann Gottlieb Rall in Trenton. Rall commanded his troops for personal glory and for money. Accordingly, his epitaph reads, "Here lies Colonel Johann Rall, for him, it is all over." But for Washington, it had just begun. Rall was a mercenary, but Washington fought for a just cause and for the right to be self-governed.

Washington displayed this trust in God during his entire life, and because of this, his faith increased throughout his life. When he finally retired from public life and did not seek a third term as president, he walked away from power. King George III, when learning of Washington's decision, stated, "[Washington's decision to yield power voluntarily] placed him in a light, the most distinguished of any man living" and that he was "the greatest character of the age" (*Founding Father—Rediscovering George Washington,* page 103). It is little wonder then that Washington wrote of the power of faith and virtue as having consequences beyond what military science could have predicted. In a Thanksgiving Proclamation in 1789, he said:

> It is the duty of all nations to acknowledge the Providence of Almighty God, to obey His will, to be grateful for his benefits, and humbly implore His protection and favor. (*George Washington's Sacred Fire,* page 207).

But the fact he considered himself a suffering, even an unprofitable servant can be seen in the following vignette. After the war was over, Congress had not paid Washington's men. After all, the United States was broke and did not have the money. His officers were upset and threatened to march on Congress. Washington received a letter from the Congress and called his officers to a meeting on March 15, 1783, at Newburgh, New York. The following is an account of what happened:

> After reading a portion of the letter with his eyes squinting at the small writing, Washington suddenly stopped. His officers stared at him, wondering. Washington then reached into his coat pocket and took out a pair of reading glasses.

Few of them knew he wore glasses, and were surprised. "Gentlemen," said Washington, "you will permit me to put on my spectacles, for I have not only grown gray but almost blind in the service of my country." In that single moment of sheer vulnerability, Washington's men were deeply moved, even shamed, and many were quickly in tears, now looking with great affection at this aging man who had led them through so much.... (*George Washington, A Biography*—Volume V, *Victory with the Help of France,* page 435).

What we see here applies directly to how we increase our faith. We see in George Washington's life that he was humble, and although he was a wealthy Virginia planter, he acknowledged the source of his leadership. It was his faith in God that provided a beacon of hope for him in the darkest of days. Washington had learned to walk to the edge of the light and then a few steps farther. Washington could not know the end from the beginning. There could be no cost/benefit analysis because the costs were uncertain and immeasurable; the benefit, should there be one was unknowable. These were only vague calculations under battle circumstances he could not anticipate.

This does not mean that cost/benefit analysis is never useful. In the right circumstances, cost/benefit analyses are completely compatible with faith, however, the suffering servant, the man who regards himself as an unprofitable servant when compared to the Lord will know when such should be applied. In matters of life and death, Washington was inspired in his plan because of the virtue found in his soul. This has nothing to do with cost/benefit. Consequently, Washington epitomized Paul's definition of faith: it is a well-grounded assurance of that for which we hope, and a conviction, due to Washington's feeding of his soul, of the reality of things we do not see.

Washington knew in his heart the plan would work for it was inspired in the realms where science and logic have no currency. Washington knew that his faith was operational because he knew that faith was the first principle of heaven and that it was by the law of faith that he had founded his plan of action. His soul was undergirded by his faith and it was by the law of faith that his deliverance was made possible. Washington acted on his plan precisely because it was conceived in faith and forged with the virtue found in his soul. He rejected the criticism of those like Charles Lee, who thought he had better skills with respect to military matters. Washington had faith in God and planned the battle with no thought of personal gain. To some it was folly, but Washington knew his men and they knew him. As a result, he moved forward with the assurance given him in faith, and was delivered a victory at Trenton.

FAITH BEYOND THE VEIL

We have learned that faith is one of the most important elements required to build a testimony, and we have further learned that faith does not come to us through obedience. The genesis of faith is found in a broken heart and a contrite spirit, which enables the true author of faith, our Savior, to grant to us His gift known as faith. Obedience, on the other hand, while not the author of faith is important because through sighted obedience our faith is made perfect. Washington's example also shows us why faith is the irrevocable law decreed in heaven upon which all blessings are predicated. Washington's example further illustrates that because he was a virtuous man, and cared very much about matters of the soul that are embraced by virtue, he demonstrated that there is a direct relationship between two of the first principles of the gospel, faith and repentance, and the ability to see the kingdom of God.

Even though Washington's life expired before the restoration of the gospel, his faith and his virtue led to the remarkable link to baptism and the gift of the Holy Ghost. Wilford Woodruff recorded the following vision given to him in 1877 in the St. George Temple:

> I will here say, before closing, that two weeks before I left St. George, the spirits of the dead gathered around me, wanting to know why we did not redeem them. Said they, "You have had the use of the Endowment House for a number of years, and yet nothing has ever been done for us. We laid the foundation of the government you now enjoy, and we never apostatized from it, but remained true to it and were faithful to God." These were the signers of the Declaration of Independence and they waited on me for two days and two nights. I thought it very singular, that notwithstanding so much work had been done, and yet nothing had been done for them. The thought never entered my heart, for the fact, I suppose, that heretofore our minds were reaching after our more immediate friends and relatives. I straightway went into the baptismal font and called upon Bro. McCallister to baptize me for the signers of the Declaration of Independence, and fifty other eminent men, making one hundred in all..." ("Discourse" *Deseret News,* 27 March 1878, pages 114–115).

In addition to George Washington and the signers of the Declaration of Independence, there were fifty other great men included, as recorded above, John Wesley and Christopher Columbus, who were also ordained high priests. Others who had their work done included Fredrick the Great, Daniel Webster, Henry Clay, Lord Byron, Edward Gibbon, Johann Wolfgang Goethe, Friedrich Schiller, Robert Fulton, Sir Walter Scott, William Wordsworth, Charles Louis Napoleon Bonaparte (Napoleon III), who had recently died in 1873. These are but a few who had developed the faith and virtue to come to the temple in St. George to have their work done (see *Collected Discourses,* vol. 3, pages 431–440).

As President Woodruff noted, there were 100 men, and none of them would have been able to attend him unless they had faith in the Lord Jesus Christ and were prepared to repent of their sins so that they could receive the ordinances of proxy baptism in St. George. President Woodruff also directed these ordinances be performed for their wives. The connection between faith and virtue is clear, as is the connection between faith and obedience. This momentous vision, which resulted in baptism and confirmation for some of the greatest men in history and their wives, could not have happened without faith. They would not have seen the kingdom of God because they would have lacked virtue. They turned their belief in Christ into faith: they allowed their faith to be increased through the love of the Savior and consequently, they were empowered by their faith.

Faith is clearly the enabling power for their obedience and thus they sought after works produced by faithful obedience, even baptism. Faith, when we understand it as a law and a principle, becomes a power that brings the Holy Ghost into our lives. We then hunger after the Spirit for we have come to know that the Holy Ghost will teach us all things we need to do (see 2 Nephi 32:3). Faith, when mixed with charity, becomes a power to move us to act in the name of the Lord. When faith is mixed with love, it then becomes redemptive faith. Accordingly, obedience rendered through redemptive faith makes our works perfect just as James taught us in James 2:22, *"Seest thou how faith wrought with his works, and by works was faith made perfect?"*

THE LAW OF FAITH IS FOUNDATIONAL TO THE SOUL

We see from the above that within virtuous souls, faith is best received and cultivated. And through their obedience in faith, eventually they will be led to embrace the first ordinances of the gospel, baptism and confirmation. Peter provided this direct link in Acts 2:38 when he taught, *"Then Peter said unto them, Repent, and be baptized every one of you in the name of Jesus Christ for the remission of sins, and ye shall receive the gift of the Holy Ghost."* We are saved through the blood of Christ in faith; we are obedient in faith and seek baptism. Do we not see now how important it is to declare this principle as disciples of the Lord? Even if a potential hearer of the word does not act today on the message, if they are virtuous or become virtuous—as did the men who came to Wilford Woodruff—the seeds of the gospel of redemption are planted in their souls.

Because we understand this, we now know there is an indirect relationship between principles and law. Lehi taught Jacob correctly in the wilderness in 2 Nephi 2:5, as we have previously noted, *"And men are instructed sufficiently that they know good from evil.... And by the law no flesh is justified...."*

So now we come to understand: it is the Spirit, not the law that justifies us before God, hence the relationship between obedience and faith is an indirect one. Do we not receive our blessings because of obedience? The answer is, indirectly, yes. It has become clear that obedience is both a principle and a practice. As we discovered earlier, faith is both a principle and a law; when we receive the gift of faith, we also receive the gift of love.

Then we have power given to us to be born of God so that the image of Christ can be engraved upon our countenances (see Alma 5:14-15). This is accomplished by bringing forth the sacrifice of a broken heart and a contrite spirit and then by binding ourselves to the Savior as shown by His example when He washed the feet of the Twelve: our desires become like His desires and our faith then perfects our works. By so doing, we live now by the law of faith, not unjustified works. We no longer seek to earn our way, for we realize that is impossible, just as Paul taught the Romans. We read in Romans 4:4, *"Now to him that worketh, the reward is not reckoned as of grace, but as of debt"* (Revised English Bible). We do not earn salvation, but receive it as a gift! Paul further taught us in Romans 3:21–22, *"But now a righteousness coming from God has been brought to light apart from any Law, both Law and Prophets bearing witness to it, a righteousness coming from God, which depends on faith in Jesus Christ and extends to all who believe. No distinction is made"* (Weymouth New Testament).

> **We do not earn salvation, but receive it as a gift**

We see that Paul considers faith to be both the foundational principle and the foundational law, as witnessed by the law and the prophets. There is no difference, meaning no difference between the principle and the law, to them that believe. Our obedience now exceeds mere conformity: it is now anchored by our faith and our love of Christ, as Paul taught, for then we are virtuous and are endowed with power.

QUESTIONS ABOUT THE LESSON

01
What makes the principle of faith into the law of faith?

02
Why did George Washington consider himself an unprofitable servant?

03
Why is virtue important?

04
Why is no flesh justified by the law?

05
When is it useful to apply a cost/benefit analysis and when is it not beneficial?

09

FAITH, LOVE, AND OBEDIENCE

As we begin to become aware that faith is a gift from God, we also begin to realize that faith and love stem from an understanding that God loves all men, and because of this, he extends to them the gift of eternal life. We learned that the gateway gift to eternal life is the gift of faith. But there are other gifts; they are explained to us in Moroni 8:8–18, Doctrine and Covenants 46 and in the Articles of Faith 1:7. These other gifts, like faith, are not awards, but gifts of the Spirit. We find a particular interest in the gift of faith recorded in 1 Corinthians 12. In verse 9 we learned that faith is a gift, and within this chapter Paul lists these gifts that cannot be earned, but received through sacrifice of a broken heart and a contrite spirit, as was faith. We read in verses 7–11, *"But the manifestation of the Spirit is given to every man to profit withal. For to one is given by the Spirit the word of wisdom; to another the word of knowledge by the same Spirit; To another faith by the same Spirit; to another the gifts of healing by the same Spirit; To another the working of miracles; to another prophecy; to another discerning of spirits; to another divers kinds of tongues; to another the interpretation of tongues: But all these worketh that one and the selfsame Spirit, dividing to every man severally as he will."*

We note from the above that the Lord will divide these gifts, as with all gifts, to demonstrate His largess to His children. They are not given as an award for conduct, but by His good pleasure to His children. Of course our conduct will enhance our ability to use these gifts He has given us, but they are truly gifts and not awards, which tells us that we should seek after the spiritual gifts we have been given. We learn in Doctrine and Covenants 46, that these gifts are given to the Church, therefore each member of the Church receives at least one of these gifts: such is the magnanimity of our Father in Heaven. Paul goes on to tell us in 1 Corinthians 13:1, *"If I can speak with the tongues of men and of angels, but am destitute of Love, I have but become a loud-sounding trumpet or a clanging cymbal"* (Weymouth New Testament). Notice that in this translation, the word "Love" is capitalized, meaning it has reference to the Savior.

Consequently, the kind of love to which we are referring is also a gift from the Savior. This means that it is not self-centered love, but soul-centered love. Further, in this verse, faith, hope, and charity are immutably linked together. This means that if we receive one gift, the others will follow as we act to receive the gift. This is the point of Charles Dickens' 1843 famous parable, *A Christmas Carol.* The well-known story is about the redemption of Ebenezer Scrooge. This selfish man was devoid of both faith and love. He loved himself and gloried in his cunning and ability to make money. The only other person he really loved—and that certainly was not in a Christ-like way—was Christopher Marley.

As the story unfolds, Marley has died and left the business to Scrooge. His clerk, Bob Cratchit is a sympathetic figure who is being paid a miserly wage and who has several children. His last child, Tiny Tim, has a disease for which the Cratchit's do not seem to have the means to treat. It becomes apparent fairly quickly that this boy will die if things continue the way they began. Even though it is Christmas, all entreaties directed toward Scrooge to contribute his resources to relieve the poor go unanswered; even his nephew's desire to show love to Scrooge is dismissed with the immortal, "Humbug!"

Ebenezer Scrooge is rehabilitated, but it takes three spirits from the transcendental world to soften his very hardened heart. These three spirits, "Christmases past, present, and future" were able to give Scrooge vision; they were to show him things as they really are so that his soul could be turned to the light. They were able to change his heart. We might say that Scrooge had a born again experience, which caused Dickens to write of him:

> Scrooge was better than his word. He did it all, and a great deal more; and to Tiny Tim, who did not die, he was a second father. He became as good a friend...and as good a man as the good old city knew...Some people laughed to see the alteration in him, but he let them laugh...that such as these would be blind anyway...he had no further intercourse with the Spirits, but lived upon the total Abstinence Principle, ever afterwards; and it was said of him, that he knew how to keep Christmas well, if any man alive possessed the knowledge of it. May that be truly said of us! And so, as Tiny Tim

observed, God bless Us, Every One! (*A Christmas Carol*, pages 78–79).

Scrooge developed a broken heart and a contrite spirit, which allowed him to "see the kingdom of God." And just as the Weymouth New Testament has explained above, it was the Savior' love, or Love, that the Spirits brought from above to Scrooge that changed his heart; they brought love, which then begot faith and hope. Through these, this gift of love became the gift of charity.

THE HIGHER COVENANT OF LOVE

In John 13:34, the Lord tells us to love one another, "as I have loved you." This is the new covenant, which departs from the Law of Moses. Thus, we see the love that is discussed in the Old Testament comes to us, as the Savior taught us in Matthew 22, by commandment (see Deuteronomy 6:4–5 and Leviticus 19:18). But as the young man and the young Pharisee were able to discern, this was not enough; this new commandment He gives us, the one found in John 13:34–35, is prefaced by a sacrifice. The Lord tells us to receive this higher love through sacrifice. This He did when He washed the feet of the Twelve. We read in John 13:6–9, *"Then cometh he to Simon Peter: and Peter saith unto him, Lord, dost thou wash my feet? Jesus answered and said unto him, What I do thou knowest not now; but thou shalt know hereafter. Peter saith unto him, Thou shalt never wash my feet. Jesus answered him, If I wash thee not, thou hast no part with me. Simon Peter saith unto him, Lord, not my feet only, but also my hands and my head."* We see here that the Savior was contrite as He washed the feet of the Twelve. This contrition demonstrated the Savior's faith, which he wished to impart to the Twelve. When we likewise bring forth the broken heart and the contrite spirit, they become the sacrifice required to produce the redemptive faith exhibited by the Savior. The love referenced in this new law or in the new commandment comes to us as a gift of the Spirit, conditioned on this sacrifice. This fact Paul knew well as he discussed the gifts of the Spirit in 1 Corinthians 12:9, *"to a third man, by means of the same Spirit, special faith; to another various gifts of healing, by means of the one Spirit"* (Weymouth New Testament). This version of the New Testament emphasizes the fact that the faith given as a gift is a special faith, a redemptive faith, so as to distinguish it from belief. This special faith is found in His kind of love—it is His faith, forged in His willingness to sacrifice for us. This special faith is given to us so that we can both see the kingdom of God and, with this gift of special faith, have power to accomplish whatever the Lord asks us to do.

This special gift of faith is directly related to our ability to love the Savior as He has loved us. It means that we begin to understand the condescension of God. Nephi plainly told the angel that he did not understand the meaning of all things, but that he did understand that the condescension of God meant the love of God for all men and women, that it spread to the hearts of men, and thus it was the most desirable gift of God, even above all things. It is in this context that the gift of special faith is placed. What is this special gift of faith? It is the sublime gift of receiving the faith and confidence the Savior has in His Father. This gift of faith comes to us as part of the higher law of love found in the New Testament. When we love one another as Jesus has loved us, we do so in the image of the Father's love for the Son. This love is then reflected as the grace of God for us as seen in the Savior's absolute commitment to us and to the Father in that He descended below all things. He did this so that we might be lifted up to the Father through the unparalleled act of the Atonement.

As we receive this special gift of faith found when we love God and rely on His works—and love our fellow man as the Savior loves us—then the Savior's image begins to be engraved into our countenances (see Alma 5:14–15). As this happens through the events of being born again, our faith becomes His faith. Thus, the special love the Lord has for us is inescapably tied to the gift of special faith He gives to us. This gift is known as redemptive faith and allows us access to His faith. It is His faith that is perfect faith, and it is His faith by which miracles are wrought. When we love God as He has loved us, our hearts now broken and our spirits now contrite, we are now in the position to receive His faith.

> **The special love the Lord has for us is inescapably tied to the gift of special faith He gives to us**

It is with this special gift of faith that our election is made sure. When we love the Lord in the same manner as He loves us, then we are able to obtain His unshakable faith in His father as we exchange our faith for His faith. When we are able to do this, and it takes perhaps a lifetime, then we come to love Him as He loves us. The first nascent steps of acquiring His love come when we are born again and see the kingdom of God. As we enter the kingdom through baptism, He gives us the Holy Ghost as a special gift, which then enables us to receive all His spiritual gifts in due time, beginning with redemptive faith.

How do we love each other as the Savior loves us? It is when we realize the Savior gave His life for us, His will being swallowed up in the will of the Father—this is the condescension of God, the Son. The Lord told us, by this shall all men know ye are my disciples, that we have love unto each other in the same way. It is by understanding how we find that special faith through the sacrifice of the things of the world—demonstrated by bringing forth a broken heart and a contrite spirit—that true obedience is forthcoming. If we find that our obedience is undertaken by mixing and matching various laws of God to desired blessings, or if we seek to avoid being punished for our sins by being obedient, we tell the Lord that we still seek to be profitable servants because of our righteous works.

With respect to our efforts, King Benjamin told us that even though we do all things commanded of us, we are yet unprofitable servants (Mosiah 2:21). And did not the Savior likewise put our works into perspective when he told the disciples that if they had done all they were commanded, yet would they be unprofitable servants (Luke 17:10)? Obedience in these circumstances is truly selfishness and that has little to do with faith or with love. We are thus trying to acquire the Savior's faith by putting Him in our debt through obedience. King Benjamin explains this folly completely in Mosiah 2:23–24, *"And now, in the first place, he hath created you, and granted unto you your lives, for which ye are indebted unto him. And secondly, he doth require that ye should do as he hath commanded you; for which if ye do, he doth immediately bless you; and therefore he hath paid you. And ye are still indebted unto him, and are, and will be, forever and ever; therefore, of what have ye to boast?"*

SELFLESS OBEDIENCE RE-ORDERS THE SOUL

It is not an easy task to sacrifice the self for the soul, but as we feel the swelling in our hearts that the events of being born again bring to us, we realize that our hearts are becoming broken and our spirits are becoming contrite. By having a broken heart and a contrite spirit, our will is likewise swallowed up in His will, and our souls begin to be re-ordered to reflect His priorities and His will. It is then that He can begin to further enlighten our minds, just as He did with Oliver Cowdery (see again Doctrine and Covenants 6:14–15). This is a constant priority in the scriptures. We need to be willing to sacrifice the transitory accessories of this world for the immeasurable riches of the world to come.

One such example comes from those Nephites who escaped with Alma from the wicked King Noah and fled into the wilderness (see Mosiah 18:34). We read in Alma 5:7 where Alma explains what happened to those who were baptized in the Waters of Mormon, *"Behold, he changed their hearts; yea, he awakened them out of a deep sleep, and they awoke unto God. Behold, they were in the midst of darkness; nevertheless, their souls were illuminated by the light of the everlasting word..."* The pattern is always the same, and it begins with a broken heart and a contrite spirit, even as those who were led away from King Noah came to understand. Once they had been enlightened, they needed to be baptized so that they could receive the Holy Ghost and enjoy His presence as part of a covenanted relationship with the Savior.

They had seen the kingdom of God as the events of their being born again had commenced, and by being able to see the kingdom, they wished to enter it. They did so by covenant, even the covenant of baptism, and then they could receive other gifts. This is just as Paul taught above to the Corinthians. They were now able to receive many gifts of that same Spirit. One of the most needed spiritual gifts is the gift of special faith, even redemptive faith. This kind of faith is that same faith Alma recognized as the kind that changes hearts and illuminates souls. This gift of redemptive faith is so important, and it comes to us as a gift and not as a commandment.

As we have seen, the commandment to love God first and our fellowman second were given to Moses as a commandment. This Old Testament correlation provided a direct association between obedience and the receipt of blessings, but at the center of the Law of Moses was love. This is why the Savior taught both the young man and the young Pharisee that the great commandment in the law was to love God first and then, second, to love our fellow man as we do ourselves. Thus, as we now understand the Law of Moses, obedience was mandated; in other words, we were to love God because He commanded us so to do, as well as love our fellowman for the same reason.

Why were we commanded to love as part of the Law of Moses? The reasons become clear when we read what the Apostle Paul told us about the Law of Moses: it served as a taskmaster to lead the children of Israel to Christ. The Lord has told us that the Law of Moses is fulfilled in Him and so we know that the law concerning faith, love, and obedience was graduated to a higher level. We read in Galatians 3:24, *"Let me put it another way. The law was our guardian until Christ came; it protected us until we could be made right with God through faith"* (New Living Translation). This translation of the New Testament makes it very clear that we now are not mandated to love God and our fellow men like we were under the Law of Moses, but instead we are invited to be obedient to God through the love Christ has for us as a new commandment, meaning it comes to us as a gift of the Spirit.

Are we still commanded to love God? Yes, of course, and likewise we are commanded to love our fellowman? Yes, indeed, but now it is part of the new commandment not underwritten by conformity to the Law of Moses. Rather, it is now to be done by the law of faith, which is an integral part of the new commandment. It now becomes clear that if it were not for faith, as noted above, we cannot be made "right with God." Without faith we cannot be born again and without faith, there can be no hope or charity either.

THE REQUIREMENT OF HIS GRACE

Ebenezer Scrooge was not forced to be obedient to the higher law; he became penitent, and as he did so, he embraced the love of God and the love of his fellowman, and then loved them as Jesus did. Nonetheless, we are not forced to be obedient, but do so instead under the new commandment; we are allowed to receive the gift of special redemptive faith given to us as the Lord's response to our sacrifice of a broken heart and contrite spirit. When we choose to receive this gift, we love God in the same way He loved us. Then we come to realize that His love for us was framed in His own broken heart. This allowed Him to condescend and step down so that He might pick us up. It was His broken heart that paved the way for our salvation and exaltation. Thus, Lehi taught us correctly that the ends of the law could only be answered unto those who have brought forth this sacrifice (see 2 Nephi 2:7).

By bringing forth the sacrifice of a broken heart and a contrite spirit, we signal to the Lord our willingness to accept the new commandment; we now love our Father in Heaven because He condescended from His throne above to send us His Son and the Son condescended to be that sacrifice. We also learned from Paul, in Romans 3:25 that the Lord, through His condescension, did forebear to punish the wicked until the day of judgment arrives. This was done through His grace and even as we accept Him through faith, as Paul directs, we also accept His grace through faith. Consequently, we now understand that His grace is unconditional and universal to both the obedient and those that choose not to be obedient because they either have no faith or are conforming to the commandments for non-virtuous reasons such as earning rewards, or are not obedient as they are rebellious.

All men have been made free to choose through His grace (see 2 Nephi 2:26–27), but the consequences of those acts that are not in harmony with the commandments of God are not yet fully executed; they are held in abeyance because of His grace. Moreover, we must accept His grace through faith. Should we not accept the grace of God, and not bring forth the sacrifices of a broken heart and a contrite spirit—the very sacrifices that bring us the gift of faith—then in a future day, the judgment of Christ will fall upon us. This day may come sooner than we think, but in the end, it will come. If we, through our faith, accept His grace, and act on this faith by receiving also His ordinances with such faith, then we receive the very kind of special redemptive faith Paul tells us we must acquire so that we might be made right with God (see again Galatians 3:24). This kind of faith must come by being born again to see the kingdom of God and by being baptized so that we can enter the kingdom and receive the gift of the Holy Ghost. Then, through this great gift, as we continue to bring forth the broken heart and the contrite spirit, we receive the necessary redemptive faith that is predicated on the new commandment of loving God like He loves us.

OBEDIENCE MAKES OUR FAITH PERFECT

We know that obedience is required, but since it is not the currency that purchases salvation, to what end is our obedience? If obedience is rendered with faith, then the works done in order to be obedient make our faith perfect (see again James 2:22). Obedience is necessary, but faith must come first. If we don't have faith, though still obedient, such obedience may be done for motives that may be less than savory, like that of "earning blessings," which is not virtuous. We also think that our obedience will bind the Lord, but when we read Doctrine and Covenants 82:10, where the Lord promises us He is bound when we do what He says, the context of binding means sealing. We are sealed by the Holy Spirit of Promise, meaning we are justified before God, not that He will give us whatever we want. If we are obedient with faith, our faith then allows us to obtain His faith, and with His faith, the Holy Ghost can tell us all things that we should do (see 2 Nephi 32: 5).

If we think that binding means forcing God to do what we want, we make a tragic mistake. When we do this, we find our obedience becomes tedious and un-nourishing. We tire of such obedience because, over time, either our hearts no longer respond to the cost/benefit analysis reserved for the self, or our hearts may be turned to pride, as the rewards of the world or the simulated benefits of rationalized faith gratify the self and overpower the soul. True faith, born of a broken heart and a contrite spirit, is a living faith. It is a nourishing faith and provides all young disciples sustenance in a world that is increasingly barren. Faith is that priceless gift that is given to those who have a broken heart; to all who are the humble followers of Christ. With that said, we can say assiduously that obedience is vital, but the Lord intended us to go beyond the Law of Moses and live a "new commandment" of love. So now we must identify how we make the love of Christ operable. It is how we are to be obedient to the new commandment to love as Christ loved, then we not only embrace the principle of faith, but through the love of Christ we make that principle into the law of faith. That law then delivers to us the power of Christ. It is through this power that we then seek for the salvation of others.

When we are obedient without faith, we likewise do not love our Lord. We fail to appreciate the Lord's comments on prayer found in Matthew 6:7–8, *"But when ye pray, use not vain repetitions, as the heathen do: for they think that they shall be heard for their much speaking. Be not ye therefore like unto them: for your Father knoweth what things ye have need of, before ye ask him."* Such is the strength of faith when it is undergirded by love, and such is the confidence we have in our Lord if we are obedient because we have faith in Him. We do not need vain repetition of words or of works; we have learned to love Him. Our love truly reflects His Love as an enabling power in our lives.

We will find that our faith, through love, becomes the assurance we seek as we strive to keep the Lord's commandments, even as the events of being born again commence deep within our soul. In this way our obedience makes our faith perfect because as we will discover, faith then leads to hope. This hope then leads us to embrace the gift of charity, the pure love of Christ (see Moroni 7:47), which then empowers our faith to reflect the vision of the Lord with respect to all things. Our gift of faith becomes redemptive faith. Is this not what happened to Scrooge? As our faith becomes redemptive, the Lord lends to us a portion of His faith and with His faith we can now access the power to do all things prudent before God.

OBEDIENCE MUST BE VOLUNTARY NOT COMPELLED

As we are born of the Spirit, we do indeed see the kingdom of God. And thus faith is, as Paul taught, the spiritual substance of being born again; these are the things hoped for, therefore being born again is the evidence of things unseen. Unseen yes, but not unfelt.

> **As we are born of the Spirit, we do indeed see the kingdom of God**

As our priorities re-order to reflect those of our Lord, our hearts swell in gratitude. We seek obedience because we want to be like Him, not because "we have to." Accordingly, obedience cannot be commanded as it once was under the Law of Moses. Joseph F. Smith taught:

Obedience must be voluntary; it must not be forced; there must be no coercion. Men [and women] must not be constrained against their will to obey the will of God; they must obey it because they know it to be right, because they desire to do it, and because it is their pleasure to do it. God delights in the willing heart (*Gospel Doctrine,* page 65).

With this in mind, let's look at Mosiah 4:6–7: *"I say unto you, if ye have come to a knowledge of the goodness of God, and his matchless power, and his wisdom, and his patience, and his long-suffering towards the children of men; and also, the atonement which has been prepared from the foundation of the world, that thereby salvation might come to him that should put his trust in the Lord, and should be diligent in keeping his commandments, and continue in faith even unto the end of his life.... I say, that this is the man who receiveth salvation, through the atonement which was prepared from the foundation of the world for all mankind..."*

As we read the rest of the chapter, it becomes clear that our obedience is rendered valid only through faith, even redemptive faith. Faith is a gift that comes to us when we make a sacrifice of a broken heart and a contrite spirit. King Benjamin then makes this point clear: our faith needs to be nourished by our obedience and not viewed as something that produces faith. If we seek to be born again in faith—as certainly we must—then our obedience strengthens faith and through such strengthened faith, we see ever so much more clearly the kingdom of God.

As we commence to embrace the experiences that lead us to be born again and to re-order our souls, faith becomes the very power that compels our obedience; it is with faith in the unseen that allows our obedience to make us holy and pure before God. As this happens, our faith becomes redemptive as it did with Scrooge; our love of our Savior is turned into charity. It is when we have such redemptive faith, received as a gift when we are born again and are filled with the pure love of Christ, that we move beyond the things we can see. For Scrooge, it required the visit of three spirits; for us, it requires that we have a broken heart and a contrite spirit. President Boyd K. Packer explains why redemptive faith is so important and why it should come with our efforts to be obedient. In an address given to Regional Representatives of the Twelve on April 1, 1977:

> (I learned this great truth from President Harold B. Lee when I was first a general authority). Elder Lee said, "Boyd, do you know what is wrong with you? You always want to see the end from the beginning." I replied quietly that I always wanted to see at least a few steps ahead. He answered... "My boy, you must learn to walk to the edge of the light, and perhaps a few steps into the darkness, and you will find that the light will appear and move ahead of you" ("Walk to the Edge of the Light," *BYU Magazine,* March 1991).

Elder Packer has explained to us the benefit of our obedience after we have faith. When we have faith and our obedience has brought us to the edge of the light, then we will be able to take those few steps further into the dark with assurance as we proceed, even if we cannot see and logic tells the self to forsake the path we have engaged. Our faith is thereby redemptive because we love and trust the Lord; we have received His gift of hope and seek to have charity, the pure love of Christ, even as we take those few steps. Soren Kierkegaard, a modern-day Christian existentialist, calls these steps the difference between subjective and objective truth. When talking about subjective truth, which we have repeatedly done in these lessons, Kierkegaard compares it to taking a "leap of faith" (see *Concluding Unscientific Postscript,* pages 208–209 and 288–291). This illogical leap into the dark, as Elder Packer suggested, is a leap that every believer must make as they receive the gift of redemptive faith.

It is in these circumstances that we seek the guidance of the Holy Ghost. And if we seek in faith, not pointing to our obedience as currency to receive His inspiration, but realizing that we through our faith have received His faith as we are born again, then we can be assured that the edge of the light will only be a saddle-point on our journey. We will realize that the edge of the light provides us discipline as we seek to walk the path of holiness in ever-greater strength. We will walk this path that leads us to our Savior with the more sure word of prophecy and we will come to know His will concerning us; we will then embrace that will even if it leads us onto paths that are difficult or sorrowful. We will find these paths especially configured so that we are purified as we exercise our special faith. We will be born of God through faith and then our obedience will both justify us and sanctify us in His presence.

REDEMPTIVE FAITH

It is then through the Holy Ghost that our works are made perfect through faith; they are then sealed with His power, even by the Holy Spirit of Promise (see Doctrine and Covenants 132:7). We have learned that without faith it is impossible to please

God, so what makes us think that our obedience, done without faith, will save us? Faith comes by bringing forth the sacrifice of a broken heart and a contrite spirit; we must have faith in order to do anything pertaining to the kingdom of God. This faith becomes redemptive when we acknowledge the connection between faith, hope and charity, or the pure love of Christ. They are gifts that come together as we are born again. Without redemptive faith, we might be totally obedient, but such obedience runs the risk of pride, which in turn will not produce the results we desire.

We need the ability to convert our faith into power, and that comes when our faith becomes empowered by love. It is in this way that our faith becomes redemptive. We now understand what Nephi taught us more clearly. We read in 2 Nephi 26:13, *"And that he manifesteth himself unto all those who believe in him, by the power of the Holy Ghost; yea, unto every nation, kindred, tongue, and people, working mighty miracles, signs, and wonders, among the children of men according to their faith."* As this faith is empowered with love, miracles and wonders follow such faith.

President J. Reuben Clark, then First Counselor in the First Presidency, in his conference address of April, 1960, stated, *"As I think about faith, this principle of power, I am obliged to believe that it is an intelligent force. Of what kind, I do not know. But it is superior to and overrules all other forces of which we know"* (Conference Report, April 1960, pages 43–44). With this faith, we can then seek the grace of God found in the further gifts of repentance—we can then be cleansed, ask and receive answers and, in short, bring to pass the Lord's work on the earth. Without faith, our behavior is not well-pleasing to the Lord, despite our obedience, because when we are obedient in this fashion, we think we can bind God's will to our own. We assume He will reward us with what we want and not necessarily what we need. Our souls need to be re-ordered; that has been clear through all the lessons thus far undertaken. The Holy Ghost is that force which overrules all other forces and is then able to remake us so that we can receive the Savior's love engraved into our countenances, as Alma taught us in Alma 5. This is why redemptive faith becomes the greatest gift, as Paul truly taught: faith, hope, and charity, but the greatest is charity because it makes our faith redemptive.

QUESTIONS ABOUT THE LESSON:

01
How did Scrooge's life change after the visit of the spirits; was he born again, and how did he receive the gift of faith?

02
What is redemptive faith?

03
How do the traits of hope and charity become part of redemptive faith?

04
Why is love of God and love of our fellowman an outcome of the born again experience?

05
Explain how one can become tired of obedience and how faith can counter this fatigue?

10

HOW DOES THE LORD APPROVE OF MY SERVICE

The goal of all service to the Lord is to feel His presence and His Spirit. What does this mean? The way the Lord shows His approval of our efforts in His cause is when He sends His Spirit to us as we serve. When we feel His Spirit with us, the sensation most often described is peace and assurance. Sometimes we feel emotional about our service, but we must be ever careful to acknowledge this fact: emotion can be a red herring—emotion can be mistaken for the Spirit and obscure the feelings of peace and assurance which are the hallmarks of His approval. Some hints that we have His approval of our efforts are these. First, our motive must be pure and be centered in bringing the work of Christ to those we serve. If we do this, we will feel His Spirit in our labors, and if we do, this is what the scriptures call being justified by Him. There is an exact description of the doctrine of justification found in Doctrine and Covenants 132:7 that we shall explore later, but for now, let us say justified service means we know we have His approval of the efforts we are now about to undertake.

We read of the need to perform our labors in accordance with the will of God in the following story of Saul found in 1 Samuel 15:17–23. I shall use the English Standard Version because it makes the point of justification more clearly. *"And Samuel said, "Though you are little in your own eyes, are you not the head of the tribes of Israel? The LORD anointed you king over Israel. And the LORD sent you on a mission and said, 'Go, devote to destruction the sinners, the Amalekites, and fight against them until they are consumed.' Why then did you not obey the voice of the LORD? Why did you pounce on the spoil and do what was evil in the sight of the LORD?" And Saul said to Samuel, "I have obeyed the voice of the LORD. I have gone on the mission on which the LORD sent me. I have brought Agag the king of Amalek, and I have devoted the Amalekites to destruction. But the people took of the spoil, sheep and oxen, the best of the things devoted to destruction, to sacrifice to the LORD your God in Gilgal." And Samuel said, "Has the LORD as great delight in burnt offerings and sacrifices, as in obeying the voice of the LORD? Behold, to obey is better than sacrifice, and to listen than the fat of rams."*

Often we explain the meaning of these verses, as "obedience is better than sacrifice." What we see, however, is that the true meaning of these verses lies in listening! Saul thought he was obedient and he was, in his own way, but not the way the Lord wanted; he ceased to be humble and thought he knew best. He thought his works, mighty as they appeared to be, would please the Lord. His obedience did not follow his faith, because he did not have faith. He had works alone; he did not listen. His obedience was done to please his soldiers, not his God. Thus, it could not be accepted nor justified. This passage of scripture is vital; we must have faith before we render our obedience. Paul explains to us why this is so in Hebrews 11:6, *"And without faith it is impossible to please God, because anyone who comes to him must believe that he exists and that he rewards those who earnestly seek him"* (New International Version). If we refuse to listen to Him, we do not seek Him. Accordingly, we refuse to have faith in Him and without faith, we behave as Saul did. Our obedience is only an effort to impress Him. He is impressed when we are humble and have faith, otherwise He cannot accept our efforts nor justify our works.

TRUE DISCIPLES SERVE WITH CORRECT MOTIVE

By adopting the correct motive, and by listening to the Lord, the young disciple will find it exhilarating to prepare to receive the gifts of the Spirit, which will then, in turn, continue to feed the soul of such a disciple for his or her entire life. The gifts the Lord is prepared to bestow on those with the correct motive are of incalculable value. Truly, Paul told the Corinthians about the value of having the correct motive when he said, *"Eye hath not seen, nor ear heard, neither have entered into the heart of man, the things which God hath prepared for them that love him"* (1 Corinthians 2:9). We learn from Paul that the purest motive for service in the Lord's cause is love of God. What does this mean? It means that we love our Savior for the sacrifice He has made to redeem us from both spiritual and physical death.

We read of this redemption in the Book of Mormon, *"For as death hath passed upon all men, to fulfil the merciful plan of the great Creator, there must needs be a power of resurrection, and the resurrection must needs come unto man by reason of the fall; and the fall came by reason of transgression; and because man became fallen they were cut off from the presence of the Lord. Wherefore, it must needs be an infinite atonement—save it should be an infinite atonement this corruption could not put on incorruption. Wherefore, the first judgment which came upon man must needs have remained to an endless duration.... O the wisdom of God, his mercy and grace! For behold, if the flesh should rise no more our spirits must become subject to that angel who fell from before the presence of the Eternal God, and became the devil, to rise no more... O how great the goodness of our God, who prepareth a way for our escape from the grasp of this awful monster; yea, that monster, death and hell, which I call the death of the body, and also the death of the spirit"* (2 Nephi 9:6–8, 10).

We must understand that redemption is achieved through His mercy and grace, not earned by our obedience

Without the Savior, all would have been irretrievably lost, and all would have been prevented from returning to our Heavenly Father. And while this might be intuitive, we must understand that redemption is achieved through His mercy and grace, not earned by our obedience.

THE IRONIES OF LIFE AND THE ATONEMENT

As the Savior becomes the subject of our faith as well as the object of it, we will begin to understand the Atonement both objectively and relationally. Consequently, we come to prize the Atonement specifically as it then embraces our own personal circumstances. Thus, the love of God is at the apex of our desires to be of service to Him. It is the purest and best motive. It has been the purpose of these lessons for a young disciple to teach those who are called to serve to come to know the Savior, in the way both Paul and Moroni taught, when they counseled us (Hebrews 12:2 and Moroni 6:4), that we should be like they are—we should look to the Lord, *"... relying alone upon the merits of Christ, who was the author and finisher of their faith."* It is when we make the Savior the subject as well as the object of our faith that the ironies of life begin to make sense; they are swallowed up in His Atonement. And as he becomes the subject of our faith as well as its object, we begin to develop an intimate association with Him that brings us peace and assurance of yet greater truth.

We will learn what this means and how this reliance on our Savior shapes other motives and focuses our intentions on the real purpose of our desire to be young disciples. In the prior nine lessons we have explored the relationship between faith, grace, works, and obedience. We have closely examined this relationship, for they are singularly tied together as an expression of God's grace contained within His sacrifice. As we come to understand the Atonement of our Savior, these doctrines will undergird our efforts as young disciples and eager servants of the Lord. As we come to understand how these four topics are

> **The ironies of life begin to make sense; they are swallowed up in His Atonement**

interrelated, we will discover that the role of the Holy Ghost and His mission is indispensable with respect to the important doctrines of justification and sanctification.

THE ROLE OF JUSTIFICATION AND SANCTIFICATION

President Ezra Taft Benson called the doctrines of justification and sanctification basic to our understanding of the Atonement. He said, "faith, repentance, baptism, the Holy Ghost, endurance, prayer, justification and sanctification through grace, and loving and serving God, provide the foundation for our desire to serve" ("A New Witness for Christ," *Ensign,* November 1984). We must know these essential truths so that we can feel our Savior's love as we serve Him. If our true motive for becoming young disciples is found in our love of Him and our realization that our own Salvation is only possible through His mercy, merits, and grace (see 2 Nephi 2:8), then we will be like Enos and seek Him to justify us through the Holy Ghost (see Enos 1:1–4). Once we feel the Lord's presence when we pray, and when we find the peace, the quiet assurance that comes to us when He is both the subject and the object of our faith, we will find it easier to let Him also be the author and finisher of our faith. This understanding comes as we seek to be justified by our faith.

Paul taught the new members of the Church, *"For the promise, that he should be the heir of the world, was not to Abraham, or to his seed, through the law, but through the righteousness of faith. For if they which are of the law be heirs, faith is made void, and the promise made of none effect.... Therefore it is of faith, that I might be by grace; to the end the promise might be sure to all the seed; not to that only which is of the law, but to that also which is of the faith of Abraham; who is the father of us all"* (Romans 4:13–14, 16). We are justified by faith, not by works without faith (Enos 1:8), and then we will be obedient for the right reasons. We learn why this is so in James 2:22, *"Seest thou how faith wrought with his works, and by works was faith made perfect."*

As we partake of the sacrament every week, we can know through His Spirit that we are on the right path. This path will eventually lead to our own sanctification, or being made holy in the blood of Christ. As we feel the justification of our lives through our faith, again like Enos, we will desire this same great blessing for our Heavenly Father's other children and this will enhance our true motive for becoming young disciples of Christ (see Enos 1:13). Then we will come to know why faith, grace, and obedience work together to undergird the doctrine of justification by faith and sanctification by the Spirit. These will be set in a context of being born again, and we will come to know why this doctrine of spiritual rebirth is so vital. It is by these doctrines that our primary motive, the love of God and the love of His children, will be refined and enhanced. We will come to know the peace that comes in living a justified life, for that life is on the path to sanctification.

UNDERSTANDING OUR RELATIONSHIP WITH JESUS CHRIST

We know that difficult days do in fact lie ahead because difficult days are even now upon us. We see the signs of the times unfolding before our very eyes. The day and the hour of His coming are not now for us to know, but we do know, and the prophets today do testify, that the signs of His coming are abundant. The time for us to build an eternal relationship with Him is at hand. We cannot build such an important relationship without tending to matters of the soul. We will never understand the Lord nor will we come to know Him if our relationship is reduced to empirical steps, charts, or "reaction formations." We find that our relationship with Him is governed by love, just as He so abundantly declared millennia ago. It is through this love of Christ that we will learn to find truth by developing our ability to learn from Him. We will find that the covenants we have made with Him will augment our love for Him because as He is the truth (subjectively), He will be viewed as the author and the finisher of our faith.

Because we will know the Truth as a being, neither as a collection of facts nor as a substance, therefore it will be the Lord Himself who will set us free from ignorance and from sin, through the ministry of the Holy Ghost. This is the doctrine of justification. It will be as He said to us in John 8:36, *"If the Son therefore shall make you free, ye shall be free indeed."* When we first seek to listen to the Spirit by being humble, we begin to see the world in the way our Lord sees it. We read in Alma 32—the Book of Mormon's excellent teaching about faith—that such an ability to see comes to us when we can first listen to the Spirit. In verse 8, Alma tells us to be humble, something that Saul lacked, which then precluded Saul's ability to listen. We read, *"I behold that ye are lowly in heart; and if so, blessed are ye."* Why are we blessed? It is because when we are humble, we listen to the Spirit. And as we listen to the whisperings of the Holy Ghost, we receive the gift of faith as taught by Paul in 1 Corinthians 12:9. We read further in Alma 32, in verse 35, *"O then, is not this real? I say unto you, Yea, because it is light; and whatsoever is light, is good, because it is discernible, therefore ye must know that it is good…"*

As we learn to listen, we then can hear the Spirit approve of our actions because we will seek such approval. This approval means our actions are justified. This justification is one of the greatest gifts a young disciple of the Lord can receive—to know from on high that the Savior approves of our efforts brings peace and quiet assurance. We read in Isaiah 32:17, *"The fruit of that righteousness will be peace; its effect will be quietness and confidence forever"* (New International Version). How do we begin to find the fruit of righteousness? How do we find confidence in our faith to listen perfectly to the Spirit? When we have been humble, we have received the gift of faith. It is now our task to magnify this gift by listening more perfectly to the Spirit in quiet effectiveness; we must listen in our hearts and not in loud and conspicuous demonstrations of alleged faith. Our confidence in Christ comes to us in small but effective ways (see Alma 37:6).

In the Weymouth New Testament's rendering of Matthew 11:29, we read, *"Take my yoke upon you and learn from me; for I am gentle and lowly in heart, and you will find rest for your souls."* In the King James Version, we read that we must learn of him. By coming to know we actually must learn from Him gives us a perspective with respect to correct motive. We cannot learn from Him unless our motives are pure, and the central motive to learn must be love of Christ. This is the reason to serve; and no other motive can replace this one. When we are prepared to learn from Him, then the words of Nephi make perfect sense. In 2 Nephi 32:5 we read, *"For behold, again I say unto you that if ye will enter in by the way, and receive the*

Holy Ghost, it will show unto you all things what ye should do." Because we are now ready to learn from Him, the libraries of heaven will be at our disposal and truth will be poured into our souls in ways that we cannot adequately explain.

Then we will find peace and rest in an eternal relationship with our Lord (see again Isaiah 32:17). We will begin to comprehend Paul's words found in Ephesians 5:2, *"And walk in love, as Christ also hath loved us, and hath given himself for us an offering and a sacrifice to God…"* In this way, we respond to the Lord's new commandment to love our fellow man, *"as I have loved you"* (See John 13:34). This is why motive is everything; with the right motive, our lives will be forever changed as we act in His service. By having the right motive to serve, we as young disciples active in the Lord's service find that our motive becomes extremely relevant and without the right motive, our time in His service is but another exercise to please the self or others. With the correct motive, the Lord will make more out of our service than we ever could. Correct motive is the key to magnification—when we are magnified by the Spirit through being justified, we are made more than we ever could be without Him. Thus let us strive in faith so our motive may be pure.

QUESTIONS ABOUT THE LESSON

01
Why does the Lord require me to first listen?

02
How does the atonement help make sense of life?

03
How is preparing the self different from preparing the soul?

04
Why does being justified require His approval of my works and how do I know I am justified before Him?

05
How do I become a true disciple?

EPILOGUE

These first ten lessons were given to young Latter-day Saints to assist them in making the decision to become a disciple of the Lord. It is a life-altering decision that comes to men and women, and it should not be made lightly or carelessly. If we undertake the Lord's way to reach a decision about discipleship, we initiate events that will lead us to the path of living water. We will begin to be born again, and we will enter upon the path that allows us to both see and enter the kingdom of God. These lessons have uncovered the absolute need for faith. We have further learned that it is impossible to please God if we do not have faith.

Let us conclude these first ten lessons by looking to Alma's discourse on faith. These lessons have emphasized the need for faith and have demonstrated a fundamental need in matters of the soul. In that light we have come to know that the law of faith is that law irrevocably decreed in heaven upon which all blessings are predicated. A fitting epitaph to this first volume is found in Alma 32. In verse 16 we find what we have learned in this volume confirmed. It is here that we read of the need to be humble, *"... blessed is he that believeth in the word of God, and is baptized without stubbornness of heart, yea, without being brought to know the word, or even compelled to know, before they will believe."* Alma confirms that humility and a broken heart and a contrite spirit are the building blocks given to fulfill the law of sacrifice.

When this happens, the Lord responds and we receive from Him the gift of faith, and as we receive the gifts of hope and charity, we receive even the gift of redemptive faith as our confidence in Him increases. As this happens, and we learn to rely solely on Him and His works to save us, Alma teaches us in verses 26 and 27, *"Now, as I said concerning faith—that it was not a perfect knowledge—even so it is with my words. Ye cannot know of their surety at first, unto perfection, any more than faith is a perfect knowledge. But behold, if ye will awake and arouse your faculties, even to an experiment upon my words, and exercise a particle of faith, yea, even if ye can no more than desire to believe, let this desire work in you, even until ye believe in a manner that ye can give place for a portion of my words."*

Alma then tells us of the experiment he wishes us to undertake. This volume coaches potential disciples on how they can commence Alma's experiment in their own lives, which will lead them to seek to be born again, to bring forth the broken heart and the contrite spirit, and to realize that obedience, without faith, is mere conformity. Readers of Volume I learn how to increase their faith. As they do so, they learn how to receive answers to their prayers and how to recognize the hand of God in their lives. These lessons are thus vital to the life of any disciple, but particularly for the young disciple. They equip anyone contemplating serving the Lord, whether on a full-time mission, a service mission or in any other service capacity. Being a disciple of Christ is a full-time effort and that effort needs to be armed with tools that feed the soul. These tools allow the love of God to fill our heart with the desire to bring to pass His work and thereby bring salvation to our soul.

Alma tells us to commence his experiment even if we have belief only, because he knows that the events of being born again will commence in our lives and we will come to know that faith is the first principle of the gospel and the law by which we come to know God. Faith is the principle that governs all action with respect to God. He then concludes his discussion on faith in verse 35, *"O then, is not this real? I say unto you, Yea, because it is light; and whatsoever is light, is good, because it is discernible, therefore ye must know that it is good...."* Faith is real because it brings light to our soul and this is good; we then can build a superstructure of faith that can feed the soul with attributes of godliness. When we do so, our faith begins to be unshakable and then we can be certain of our decision to serve the Lord. It is an exciting time to serve, and making the right decision for the right reason will undergird our service in the Lord's kingdom for the rest of our lives.

BIBLIOGRAPHY

Alden, John R. *George Washington, A Biography.* New Jersey: Wings Books – Random House Value Publishing Inc., 1995

Ballard, M. Russell. "Missionary Work. From and Address given at the University of Utah Institute of Religion, 15 October 2006.

Benson, Ezra Taft "A New Witness for Christ." *Ensign.* Salt Lake City: The Church of Jesus Christ of Latter-day Saints, November 1984.

_____ . "Beware of Pride." *Ensign.* Salt Lake City: The Church of Jesus Christ of Latter-day Saints, May 1989.

Brookhiser, Richard. *Founding Father – Rediscovering George Washington.* New York: The Free Press- A Division of Simon & Shuster, Inc., 1996.

Conference Reports of the Church of Jesus Christ of Latter-day Saints. Salt Lake City: The Church of Jesus Christ of Latter-day Saints, April 1960.

Dickens, Charles. *Charles Dickens' Work—Child's History of England and Miscellaneous.* Boston: DeWolfe, Fiske, & Co. Publishers, 1886.

Fast, Howard. *The Crossing.* Trenton, New Jersey: New Jersey Historical Society, 1989 and "General Washington at Trenton and Princeton, December and January – A Hundred Years Ago," *Potter's American Monthly,* vol. VIII, no. 61, January 1877.

Fischer, David Hackett. *Washington's Crossing.* New York: Oxford University Press, 2004.

Freeman, Douglas Southall. *George Washington: A Biography –* Volume V, *Victory with the Help of France.* New York: Charles Scribner's Sons, 1952.

Frost, Robert. *The Poetry of Robert Frost.* New York: Holt, Rinehardt and Winston, 1969.

Jesse, Dean C. Ed. *The Papers of Joseph Smith,* vol. I. Salt Lake City: Deseret Book Company, 1989.

Kaku, Michio. *Einstein's Cosmos: How Albert Einstein's Vision Transformed Our Understanding of Space and Time.* New York: W. W. Norton and Company Publishers, 2004.

Kimball, Spencer W. Conference Report, Munich Area Conference, 1973 as reported in *Doctrine and Covenants and Church History Seminary Teacher's Resource Manuel.* Salt Lake City: The Church of Jesus Christ of Latter-day Saints, 2014.

Kipling, Rudyard. "Recessional." *A Choice of Kipling Verse.* Toronto: McMillian Co. of Canada at St. Martin's House, 1942.

Lillback, Peter A. *George Washington's Sacred Fire.* Bryn Mawe, Pennsylvania: Providence Forum Press, 2006.

Millet, Robert L. and Joseph Fielding McConkie, *The Life Beyond.* Salt Lake City: Bookcraft, 1986.

Monson, Thomas S. "Who Honors God, God Honors," *Ensign.* Salt Lake City: The Church of Jesus Christ of Latter-day Saints, November 1995.

_____. "A Call of Duty." *Ensign.* Salt Lake City: The Church of Jesus Christ of Latter-day Saints, May 1986.

Oaks, Dallin H. "Have You Been Saved?" *Ensign,* Salt Lake City: The Church of Jesus Christ of Latter-day Saints, May 1998.

Packer, Boyd K. "What Every Missionary Should Know." Address given at Mission President's Seminar, June 26, 2002.

_____. " The Great Plan of Happiness and Personal Revelation, *CES Fireside Address* given on November 9, 1993. *Missionary Preparation Manuel.* Salt Lake City: The Church of Jesus Christ of Latter-day Saints, 2005.

_____. "The Edge of the Light," *BYU Magazine,* Provo, Utah: March 1991.

Porter, Bruce D. "A Broken Heart and a Contrite Spirit," *Ensign,* Salt Lake City: The Church of Jesus Christ of Latter-day Saints, November 2007.

Pratt, Parley P. "Proclamation," *The Latter-day Saints' Millennial Star,* vol. 5, March 1845).

Smith, Joseph F. *Gospel Doctrine – The Sermons and Writings of*

Joseph F. Smith. Salt Lake City: Deseret Book Company, 1969.

Smith, Joseph Fielding. *Doctrines of Salvation.* 3 Vols., Comp. Bruce R. McConkie. Salt Lake City: Bookcraft Publishers, 1954-1956.

Solzhenitsyn, Alexander I. *The Gulag Archipelago 1918-1956 – An Expression in Literary Investigation I-II.* New York: Harper & Roe, Publishers, 1973.

Talmage, James E. *Jesus The Christ.* Salt Lake City: The Church of Jesus Christ of Latter-day Saints, 2006

Taylor, Charles. *The Sources of the Self – The Making of the Modern Identity.* Cambridge, Massachusetts: Harvard University Press, 1989.

Welch, Myra Brooks. "The Touch of the Master's Hand," *The Gospel Messenger.* Elgin, Illinois: The Church of the Brethren Press, 1921.

Woodruff, Wilford. "Discourse" *Deseret News.* Salt Lake City: The Church of Jesus Christ of Latter-day Saints, 27 March 1878.

_____. *Selected Discourses Delivered by President Wiford Woodruff, his Two Counselors, The Twelve Apostles and Others.* 5 Vols. Brian H. Stuy Ed. Burbank, California: B. H. S. Publishing, 1989.

ABOUT THE AUTHOR

Dr. William Hayes Pingree has spent his life teaching young disciples the doctrine of the gospel, leading a successful life preparation course to hundreds of young men seeking to enter the mission field. The recipient of multiple teaching awards, including the ASUU Professor of Choice Award. Dr. Pingree taught political theory (philosophy) and international relations at the University of Utah for over 20 years and was also an instructor at the LDS Institute of Religion for over 10 years.

Prior to teaching, his professional career included being appointed as senior advisor to the National Security Council under the Reagan Administration. He continues to advise politicians and senior government officials, having been the Associate Historian for the Romney Readiness Project. An author, contributor to numerous conferences, seminars and publications, Bill has found joy in raising his children after losing his sweetheart, Rose Anne, at an early age.

These lessons are based upon the principles taught to over hundreds of young men in his highly desired life preparation course.

www.ingramcontent.com/pod-product-compliance
Lightning Source LLC
Chambersburg PA
CBHW071614080526
44588CB00010B/1129